# A SECOND *Chance*

## And then some

**RUSS SCANNAVINO**

Copyright © 2024 Russ Scannavino.

All rights reserved. No part of this book may be reproduced, stored, or transmitted by any means—whether auditory, graphic, mechanical, or electronic—without written permission of both publisher and author, except in the case of brief excerpts used in critical articles and reviews. Unauthorized reproduction of any part of this work is illegal and is punishable by law.

ISBN: 979-8-89419-130-0 (sc)
ISBN: 979-8-89419-131-7 (hc)
ISBN: 979-8-89419-132-4 (e)

Because of the dynamic nature of the Internet, any web addresses or links contained in this book may have changed since publication and may no longer be valid. The views expressed in this work are solely those of the author and do not necessarily reflect the views of the publisher, and the publisher hereby disclaims any responsibility for them.

One Galleria Blvd., Suite 1900, Metairie, LA 70001
(504) 702-6708

# Preface

---

I was young, just 23 at the time of my wreck and I thought I had the world saying yes to me. I earned rapid success at the company I was working for. In a little more than three years I went from a part-time employee to one of the top managers in the company, if not the best manager in the company. I had won the contest for the best store appearance to the customers (which included the merchandise that would sell as well as no empty shelf space), two out of three years. I heard that the reason my store did not win it the third year was because I did not have my managers "smock" on. This was a red jacket that the managers wore to distinguish themselves from the other employees. Not a bad, quick, track record for a young manager. I was the youngest person ever to make manager, another one of my accomplishments I accomplished in my short tenure.

During the time of my accomplishments, I was also taking home "good" money, especially for a 23 year old male. I already had one sports car, a 1968 Camaro Z-28 which my brother had fixed up really nice for me, (he was a mechanic). It had buttoned-tucked interior with 4:88 gears in the rear-end. Along with that my brother had built a really fast engine for it. It also had an automatic transmission with a "slip-kit" in it. It was the only street car I had seen that could pull the front wheels of the ground. It was fast. It was a classic, but that wasn't enough. Remember I was enjoying all kinds of success with my job and along with the success came the "status symbols" I had to get to show my achievements to who ever would look. Pretty stupid I know but like I said, I was only 23 years old and although I was enjoying success I did not understand the way to show it or if I had to show it.

I had an exceptional assistant manager who was older than I was and always gave me advice, it's just that I thought I did not need any advice.

He saw the potential in me and asked me to go downtown with him to his "alma mater", which happened to be a college named Tulane University which has an excellent reputation. After visiting the campus with him and we were driving home he brought up the subject of me going back to college, I already had two years of college credits from when I went to school before I started working. He told me that he would pay the first years tuition for me if I decided to go back.

That was like a brick hitting me in the face. An employee of mine offering to pay my first years tuition at an expensive college, even if it would have been a junior college, that's quite a compliment.

Like I said, my assistant manager was older than I was and he was very well educated. His name is David and from that day forward I looked at David in a different way. We had a great working relationship but now I saw in him the belief that he had in me.

I was shocked and stunned and surprised at what had happened to me.

My father had always told me to think before I say something or make a decision, but I still didn't. I told David that I had a job that I liked and that I planned on retiring from the company. I thanked him.

Can you imagine? A 23 year old kid making a decision that would affect the rest of his life in 5 minutes. Now I know how important those words were that my father told me.

We continued working and winning contest and there was another contest. This one dealt with the managers of all the stores, who already had a good base pay, having money added on to the base pay by way of money that you won added to your base pay. The way it worked was that your supervisor would inspect your paperwork your payroll and your inventory etc, for each part of the inspection that you got right you were given a certain sum of money that would be added to your base pay, sort of like a professional football players contract with incentives, if they achieve those incentives they earn more money.

On this inspection, I received the most money added to your base pay, which means I got all the parts of the inspection correct. So I made more money.

I'm telling you this not to brag but to show you the success I was enjoying and how I was feeling, like I could conquer the world, which I could not.

As good as my life was going at this time, it came to a sudden stop at 2:30 in the morning on October 19th, 1983. It came to such an unexpected halt that it would be 2 years before I enjoyed that kind of success again. Not only my work success but my relationship's with girls. If I would not have had my accident, I would not have married my wife, would not have had our two children; my life would be completely different.

This book will show you how I changed and show you that it wasn't me who did the changing, but GOD who did the changing in me.

# Chapter One

~~~~~~~~oooooo~~~~~~~~

It was Friday, November 19th, 1983.

It was a day I'll never forget, and rightly so.

I got off of work at 4:00 pm as was usual for a Friday afternoon. I went home and washed and waxed my car. It was a nice looking car that I loved and loved to drive around in and get stares. After I finished with my car I went inside and took a shower and got dressed to go out, which was usual for a Friday evening for me. After talking to my parents for a while, I called my friend Richie and asked him if he wanted to go get a few drinks than grab something to eat. He declined and said that there was a boxing match coming on T.V. that he wanted to watch and that I could come over and watch it with him if I wanted.

That wasn't what I had in mind.

I declined and went to a bar by myself and got a few drinks and wasted some time. At around 9:00 I went to the K Mart where my present girlfriend worked and just walked around looking at things waiting for her to get off work. She worked in the office and when the store closed at ten o'clock, she was able to leave without doing any cleaning up.

When the store closed, we left in separate cars to go out for a while. We went to a lounge where they also served food and we had a few drinks, just talking about the day and how things were going with each other.

It was a quiet night by my standards and after talking for a few hours, 4 1/2 to be exact, and having a few drinks, we decided to call it a night since I had to go to work at 6:00 the next morning.

A few hours of sleep was usual for me; I was young and relatively strong and I didn't need that much sleep. I would go some nights with only three hours of sleep, but what the heck, I thought I was invincible (you'll see what I mean as we go along).

We finally left the bar, she in her car and me in mine. I asked her if she wanted me to follow her home to make sure she got there alright. I always thought about the other person and how I could help them out and I would have offered that to Richie if we were together in separate cars, that's just the way I am.

She said no, that I should go home and get some sleep because I looked tired and that was the truth.

In a way I was relieved.

We went down the highway about 100 yards were I was going to turn right and she was going to go straight. We stopped for the red light and waited; it seemed for an eternity. While we were waiting I lit a cigarette and put a cassette in my tape player since there weren't any C.D. players back then. I remember it was either Phil Collins or Genius. I was a big fan of both the band Genius and Phil Collins and listened to both of them a lot.

The light finally turned green and I watched her go straight before I turned right.

I proceeded to go down the street, which was 2 lanes divided by a neutral ground with 2 more lanes going in the opposite directions on the opposite side of the neutral ground.

I went down the street around 50 yards, I was in the left hand lane, and a big pickup truck, which was going very fast, had run the stop sign on the other side of the street and then ran the stop sign that was in the neutral ground and ran right smack in my drivers door. He hit me perfectly in the drivers door, not one inch to the back or one inch to the front. He pushed my around 25 yards into the yard of a guess who? A lawyer, kind of ironic.

I know he was speeding because he pushed my car so far.

That shows you what kind of story this will be, but I can say that it is all true.

After hitting me and obviously causing a lot of noise, the driver simply backed up his truck, straightened out and proceeded to go where ever he was going.

Can you imagine! For all the other driver knows, he just killed someone and he just backs up his truck and goes on his merry way, like nothing serious happened.

Ironically, at 2:35 in the morning, someone had scene the accident and got the license number of the truck and luckily for me had called "911".

That was omen #1, that someone had witnessed the accident AND called "911".

The police and the fire department came to the scene of the accident. The fire department couldn't get me out of the drivers door because there was no more drivers door. The drivers seat was around 2 inches wide from the impact of the truck hitting the car.

The drivers door was jammed shut from the impact of the collision.

The passenger door was jammed and would not open from me hitting it. Luckily my friend Richie was not with me or he or/ and I would be dead. Luckily for me, my car had a sunroof which happened to come in handy at that time.

The ambulance drivers were able to get me out through the sunroof.

The police had the drivers license number and looked up the drivers address and went to his house, which happened to be about 1/2 of a mile away and arrested the driver of the truck at his house.

Luckily, I did not have my seat belt on or I would not be righting this book, if you know what I mean. If I had my seatbelt on I would have died because the drivers seat was two inches wide.

That was omen #2.

That should show you the kind of shape my car was in.

Luckily or unlucky, depending on how you look at it, I was in a coma and don't remember anything, I don't even remember seeing the truck before it hit me.

I was put on a stretcher and strapped down and put in the ambulance and brought to the hospital.

At the hospital they got my wallet out of my pants and looked for identification. Luckily my wallet with my drivers license was still in my pocket and they were able to determine who I was and call my parents. Luckily, no one else but my brother who also lives close by, has my last name in the state. They would have been calling all these people before they were able to get my parents on the phone if I had a common name.

That was omen # 3.

I remember my mother telling me that my father told my mother that the hospital called and that my father had answered the phone and the person at the hospital said that they should come over because I was involved in an auto accident. My father told my mother that I was involved in an accident and had probably broken my leg.

My father got dressed and went to the hospital at around 3:00 in the morning.

Was he in for a surprise when he got to the hospital!

All my jewelry, money and clothes were gone; I was dressed in a hospital gown with all kinds of tubes running out of my body; I looked as though I was asleep.

My father did not know what happened to me yet but was about to find out.

The doctor who was assigned to me was on call and he must have been at home when the hospital called him and told him that there was a patient coming in with a head injury, which I will tell you about in a minute; was dressed in street clothes with a hat on, and I remember my mother telling me that my father told her that he looked like the T.V. character "Columbo". He tells my father that I was involved in a car accident and was in a coma and had suffered a "closed- head injury". A closed head injury is an injury that happens inside your head, thus a closed head injury.

The force of my car getting hit by the pick up truck and smashing me into the passengers side door sent my brain back and forth inside my head, like a scrambled egg.

The doctor told my father that the left side of your brain controls the right side of your body and the right side of your brain controls the left side of your body. He said that my brain was swollen and that I was having trouble breathing and that was the reason he had me on a breathing machine. He said that he didn't know when the swelling in my brain was going to go down and that there was nothing my father could do at the hospital so he should go home and collect his thoughts and tell my mother what happened.

A younger doctor with less experience might have decided to give me a tracheotomy to help with my breathing. That was omen # 4, not having them cut a whole in my throat to help me breathe.

This is a view of the front of my car.

The inside of my RX-7.
My assistant managers car sitting next to mine.

A view from the top. Notice the rearview mirror.

It's a good thing I didn't have my seatbelt on, or I wouldn't have been able to write this book.

# Chapter Two

-∞∞∞-

My father went home and told my mother what had happened to me, (my father still did not know what kind of accident I was in, if I hit someone or if I ran into a tree or if someone hit me), and he said that it did not look good for me.

They made some coffee and sat down to try and collect their thoughts. my father told my mother what had happened to me (that I was involved in a car accident) again.

My father poured himself some coffee.

The first person my mother called was a religious friend of hers that she had met at a prayer meeting. My mother is very religious. She knew that he worked at the Post Office and that he would be getting ready to go to work. She told him what had happened to me and he was in shock. They started praying for me on the phone.

I know that prayers helped a lot in my recovery, prayer's were said for me by all the priests I knew and my family and friends and my families friends friends

By 7:00 a.m. my parents had called all of my family, who happened to live in different states. My mother did not call any of my friends, she only called family. She also had to call my assistant manager and told him what had happened to me and that he would have to go and open up the store for me.

The store was supposed to open up at 6:00 a.m.

My assistant managers name was David Eguidan and he and my parents had become good friends. That was the only friend/working associate she had called and you'll see what happens. It still amazes me!

David starts crying on the phone because David thought the world of me.

David goes and opens the store for me, on time, and all the people who normally come in expecting to see me saw David instead. I worked every Saturday morning. Well, I became friends with a great many of the customers and David knew the ones I knew so he told the ones who knew me what had happened to me. They were all shocked to hear that I was in a coma and would not be coming to work.

David told me that they all left in disbelief, telling their friends. That is how ALL the friends I had found out about my accident. Friends I hadn't seen or talked to in years found out.

At noon that day there were so many people at the hospital to see me even though they couldn't go in intensive care to see me, that the nurses were shocked at the sight of so many people. They told my parents that they had never seen so many people at a hospital to see one person. I was kind of a celebrity it seemed.

From that day on there was always DIFFERENT people at the hospital.

A friend of mine, Fr. Greg Aymond, came to the hospital quite regularly to see me and he also came to the second hospital, the rehabilitation hospital after he said mass on Sunday to give me communion. He is a truly special person.

He was also one of the priest who married my wife and I and later on became an Archbishop.

We had three priests say our marriage and all three were monsignors at the time. Later on one became a Bishop and the other became an Archbishop while the third retired.

Well, the swelling in my brain did eventually go down so it was good that I did not receive the tracheotomy and after 12 days I finally woke up from my coma. Everybody was on a 'high'. I did not recognize anybody at first and when I did start talking you could not understand what I was trying to say, my speech was so bad.

Well, one of my ex- girlfriends heard about my accident and she was coming to the hospital regularly to see me, and along with my present girlfriend and various friends and family, it was a jam-up situation.

The ex-girlfriend and I went out for four years and my parents knew her well. They adored her. My present girlfriend, my parents did not really know that well. My parents, being stressed out from their son being in a coma and not knowing what the future held for me, talked to my ex- girlfriend a lot when she was there. She was adorable.

Her name was Angel and she was thought of like an angel by my parents.

To add stress to a stressful situation, my present girlfriend asks my ex-girlfriend what she was doing there when they were both there at the same time. There were all kinds of my friends there, past and present, girls and boys, and my present girlfriend asks my former girlfriend what she was doing there? Really jealous I guess. Can you imagine?

I was told by a friend of mine who happened to be at my house talking to my parents one day, that the phone had rang and my father had answered it. When my father hung up the phone he told my mother that it was one of my present girlfriends friend who had called saying that they (my parents) were putting my present girlfriend through hell. I don't know what that was supposed to mean, but here is a parents son in a coma, coming out of the coma and his parents not knowing what the future held for him, it seems to me that they were going through hell as it was.

That takes nerve to do something like that, a lot of nerve. I'm glad I did not marry her and if it weren't for my accident I probably would have. Everything has a reason, whether you know the reason or not.

That's just my way of thinking and I think it holds a lot of weight.

There was a reason why I had my accident and I think I know part of the reason, and I can tell you that it was a good reason.

Almost getting killed in a car accident is not a good reason, bu it certainly was good because it stopped me from doing something very foolish, a lot of things. I was living my life for the day and not thinking about tomorrow seriously.

I almost got killed in my accident and my family went through hell with the whole ordeal, although they would never admit it. Imagine, a parents son, laying in a coma, and my girlfriends friend calling my parents and telling them that they were being too hard on her! They should have been consoling my parents!

That just shows you the kind of personality some people don't have.

Anyway, back to me. People had been sending the hospital cards and flowers and coming to see me and my parents. Well my mother had been keeping a log from day one of who had come to see me at the hospital and what time they came. I think the reason she did that was so I could look back and be grateful for the numerous friends who came to see me. It was a pretty smart thing to do and something only a mother would think of. I am grateful that she did that and appreciate the prayers she personally had said for me.

I finally recognized my parents and after a few days. I recognized pretty much everyone in a week.

My days at that hospital were pretty much fixed as to what I was able to do. I remember in the morning they worked with me on my walking. I had to try and walk in- between two bars holding on. I would only try and go about 20 yards but that took me around 20 minutes to do. Then they would roll me back to my room on a stretcher and I would rest or take a nap. Then at around 12:00 I would eat lunch and after that the neurosurgeon would come in and check on me. The swelling in my head finally started to go down, which was a good sign. I was right on schedule for recovering, whatever the schedule was.

I remember also that I would go across the street and see the audiologist for my hearing, which was severely damaged from my accident.

I remember once, I was laying in bed and I had to go to the bathroom. My father happened to be there and he said "why don't you try and walk to the bathroom". Well, I tried. Holding on to my father I went to the bathroom, which was only 4 feet away and then I walked back to my bed. Remember, I still did not walk by myself and they had to roll me on a stretcher to move me. Well, my neurosurgeon heard about my father telling me to try and walk and he came in and immediately gave my father a stern talk about when I will be able to walk, that they had to let nature take it's time and that my body STILL needed time to recover. That talk made my father leave my recovering to the doctors. He was just doing what a father would do. A father would want his son to walk again.

The afternoon was pretty much my free time, if you will. I would talk to my friends who came to see me and sleep when I was alone, and all this time my parents still did not tell me about my accident, what happened to me. In fact, till this day, I don't remember anyone telling me what happened to me or why I was in the hospital, why I couldn't walk or talk, or why the right side of my body didn't work like it used to.

Somehow, I knew that I was in a car accident that was not my fault, I don't how, I just sensed it. If the accident would have been my fault, my recovery possibly would have been hampered by my feeling guilty, who knows.

The whole purpose of this book is to show people who have been set back because of an injury or some kind of accident, that anything can and does happen, no matter if you recognize what is happening or not.

I recovered pretty much all the way except for my hearing, which was terrible, while other people who I have met and had an accident haven't recovered as well. That is something I can't figure out and probably never will, but with the help of GOD, anything is possible. Good things can and will happen, no matter if you know the reason or not. Certain things have happened to me that I don't know the reason why. Here's an example.

One time my wife and I moved to another house and things were going pretty good for us. Then after two years a real weird family moved next to us. Weird because they never talked to anyone, trying to make friends in a new neighborhood, and they sheltered their kids. The father was like a 270 lb. 6 foot bully. We could never figure him or his family out but to make a very long story short, we moved. I know the man-boy thinks he made us move, but my wife and I were looking for another house that my parents could live at long before the episode with the man-boy started.

This man-boy punched me and knocked while I was walking the dog one day. I was walking my dog and had to pass in front of his house, that's when the jerk punched me, AND the block captain, who I thought of as a friend, thought I fabricated the whole story.

He knocked me out cold. I'm lying on the ground in front of his house.

I could never figure that one out. I am a nice person, why did this happen to me. It happened to me to make me a better person and a better family man, because the man-boy affected my whole family. I could devote a whole chapter to that man-boy and his family, like when my family and I invited there children (2 girls and boy) but it would just bring back bad memories. He was jealous of me why I don't know but enough of that.

Remember that bad things happen to good people. I know I'm a good person.

The purpose of this book is to show you that you have to keep trying, no matter what happens to you. Times get hard, they were hard for me, and times are good like they have been most of the time for me.

Every Sunday, a priest friend of mine would come to the second hospital I went to and give me communion.

That was a very good thing for me.

This was the priest who married my wife and I. A priest, MonsignercRay Hebert gave me a job at the rectory during the summer when I was in high school, cutting the grass and doing different odd jobs, he also came to see me. I remember my mother telling me that I asked him who was cutting the grass for him now at the rectory. That was 5 years ago that I used to cut his grass.

Anyway, back to my story. After around 1 month, I was to be transferred to another hospital. This hospital was strictly a rehabilitation hospital. At that time, people from different states would go to that hospital for rehabilitation. It had an excellent reputation of rehabilitating people.

They had a T.V. commercial and one of the things they said was "we rebuild lives". They certainly did mine and I will and can testify to that.

Well, the day I was to be transported there, the receptionist told my mother that she had to pay a large amount of money for my services, and at that time they were strapping me in to the ambulance to bring me to the second hospital. I had insurance from my job that was covering the whole amount. My mother just happened to see the social worker who was assigned to me (another sign). Everyone with a head injury is assigned a social worker. She told him what the receptionist was saying and how rude she was being. He told my mother to wait a minute and he went and talked to the women. He came out a few minutes later and said he told the lady everything was being taken care of by my insurance company, and that I should be free to go, she just had to sign some release papers on me. She went back in and the lady did a 180 degree turn for the better. She talked very nice and polite to my mother. The lady never apologized to my mother for the way she spoke to her, but I guess that's where having CLASS comes in. I wish I was well at the time because I would have told that lady something, but if I would have been well I wouldn't have been at the hospital, right.

The next hospital was around 18 miles away, across the river in a different city, and you had to drive on the interstate to get there. That was simply out of the question. My mother did not drive on the interstate and my mother didn't know her way across the river. The ambulance driver let my mother ride with me in the ambulance, and that was a big break for my mother.

You can begin to see how different things worked out for my mother.

My mother always told me that if you stay close to GOD, HE will stay close to you. How true!

So I remember getting there at around 10:30 in the morning and they had to take me out of the ambulance and put me in a wheelchair. That was simply not going to cut it by my standards. I did not want to go around in a wheelchair. That afternoon, I was walking. I don't mean walking like I was O.K., but I was getting around without the wheelchair or a walker or a cane, pretty amazing I think. The next day is when they started assessing my condition, to see what kind of rehabilitation I needed.

There I went to different kinds of rehab classes like seeing if I could do math (to see if I could concentrate) if I could get along with other people etc.. I don't know exactly how, but they rebuilt my life, by the time I left I could walk again and I was able to socialize again.

When I was there, I said to myself, why do I have to do this, but like I said, there is a reason for everything, whether you know the reason or not.

They had me trying to do things that I could not do BUT I think it was to see how I would react to it, would I get frustrated and give up.

I was there for about two months and at the first hospital for one month, for a total of three months. Not bad considering they did not know if I was going to live or to what the extent my injuries would be, and also not knowing how my memory would turn out since people with head injuries often have their memory affected. I thought my memory was fine but in fact it wasn't.

Real quick, when I started going out with this girl when I was released from the hospital and finally could drive, I would always say I would call her when I got home from her house, but I always forgot to call her in the 15 minutes it took me to go home. That's just an example of how bad my short term memory was.

My parents talked to the administrator of the hospital and they were allowed to take me home for a few hours every Sunday.

So the first Sunday I went home, I was able to see my car, which was still parked in the driveway.

My mother had not wanted my car to be there because she did not know what to expect from me, how I would respond to seeing it.

It had not been taken away by the insurance company yet and as we pulled up and parked we all got out of the car in total silence. My parents didn't know what to say AND I surely didn't know what to say. I did not even look at my car as we all walked inside. After we were inside for a few minutes in complete silence, I went outside with the objective of looking at my car, by myself. I was able to actually see and study it; what a mess, seeing the blood on the seat and floor, how could anybody survive a wreck like that, I thought.

I walked around the car and looked inside. I saw what was left of the drivers seat, the whole two inches of it. The width of the drivers seat was two inches wide! The car was in a "u" shape. The impact of getting hit so hard directly in the drivers side door had bent the car into almost a "u" shape. There was still a pint of Wild Turkey in the back seat, which I drank, and still the cassette tapes in the compartment in between the front seats, but the outside of the car was a mess. The headlights were broken from the impact. To think, the day I had my accident, I washed and waxed my car that afternoon!

After about 15 minutes I went back inside. No body said anything, my parents or me. It was like they were waiting for me to say something and I couldn't.

I was glad to be alive and walking around, even if it was slow, but I was shocked at the sight of my car. How could anyone survive that?

There was a guy who lived across the street who was about my age and he had an old truck that he had fixed up. My parents told me that when the car was brought to their house, he helped them by taking certain things off the car before the insurance company had a tow truck come and take the car away, the stereo and alarm and the front bra over the headlights (as of yet they haven't taken my car away). So I walked across the street to his house and thanked him for helping my parents out and I told him that he could come over and take the stereo and burglary alarm and anything else he wanted. That was my way of thanking him for helping my parents out.

It was a very expensive stereo system and alarm but I didn't need them anymore.

So it was time to go back to the rehabilitation hospital; so soon I thought.

The time flew by and I had to go back because they only allowed me a few hours.

My mother thought that by me seeing my car I would be really upset but it didn't affect me. It was nothing to me, it didn't mean anything to me, I was just glad to be alive but now I did not have a car.

My car was a really nice looking car that I was going to put in the car show later that month. I was pretty sure that I would have won first place in the division I would have entered it in, that's all that bothered me. I had a nice looking car, one that I had fixed up to look really nice but now, that was all history.

Let me tell you this. I had another car also. Yes, a 23 year old boy who had 2 cars. My other car was a 1968 Camaro that I had put Z-28 emblems on. It had black buttoned tucked interior. I had just recently had it painted pearl white, it had a spoiler on the back, it had a 350- 4-bolt main engine that my brother had built for me that was really fast, it had 4:88 rear gears and a slip kit, Holley carburator to name a few things. In time I was going to have my friend paint blue flames on. It was the only automatic transmission street car I have seen that could pull the front wheels off the ground. It also was a nice looking and fast car. It was a classic car, but now that's history also.

Listen to why it's history.

I sold it to a friend of mine, a guy who grew up next door to me. He wrecked it the same place, the same day of the week and about the same time. He was coming home from work. That car was also totaled just like mine was.

He had his wreck two weeks before mine.

THAT'S PRETTY STRANGE.

Why I sold it, I still do not know why, but I've made my share of mistakes in life and that was just another one and one I will never forgive myself for doing.

My 1968 Camaro that pulled the front wheels off
the ground. It had a 4:88 rear end and
an automatic transmission.

Me as a senior in high school.

My mother and father with me when
I graduated from high school.

# Chapter Three

So now you know that I had two very nice cars, very good looking cars, two very fast cars both of which were totaled on the same day of week, approximately the same time and both were totaled TWO weeks apart. Strange indeed. The cars were totaled at the same place, the same time of the day, the same day of the week. You also know that I was in the first hospital for about a month, had a coma, and then went to the rehabilitation hospital for about two months.

At that hospital, I was quickly becoming bored. Why? they were simply rebuilding my life like the T.V. commercial said. There was just one thing wrong. I didn't THINK I needed my life rebuilt. I thought my life was fine, I thought I had recovered enough. I thought I could go back to work the next day. I would still have the same girlfriend and life would go on as it was, normal with out a worry about tomorrow from me.

Shows you how much I know.

That was half the problem, me thinking I could go back to work. That showed the staff at the hospital that I wasn't ready to go back home, that I wasn't as fine as I thought.

So I continued to go to my rehabilitation classes every day. I continued to go home on Sunday for a few hours and I still thought everything was fine.

I started asking all the people who were assigned to me when I could go home.

They knew I wanted out of there!

After weeks of constantly asking them, they figured they would give me a test and see if I was ready to leave. Finally, but I still had to do good on the test they were giving me.

I passed the test and they had a meeting with all of my doctors, my social worker, my parents, and myself. All of the arrangements were made for me to be released. My social worker had to call the local junior college where I was going to go and continue my rehabilitation. It really wasn't that long since my accident that I was going back home. Three months to be exact.

All of the staff at the hospital told me that I did a fast recovery, I wasn't finished my recovery, there was a lot more recovery to be done at home. More than I thought. I still was very self conscience about my speech, having people hear me, I didn't think I sounded right, the whole right side of my body was weak and I had a hard time hearing. I thought I was finished recovering, yeah right!

So, they released me at my urging and my social worker worked out the arrangement's for me to continue my rehabilitation at the junior college.

I'm getting a little bit ahead of myself. First of all, I told you that there was still a lot of rehabilitation to be done by me. First, my speech. My father suggested that I go in a quiet place in our house and practice reading to myself, out loud. That would do two things. First I would hear what my speech sounded like. I could correct the parts that needed to be corrected, practice my speech. Second, my speech would eventually get better by repetition of constantly reading. So I went in my backyard, since I was still self-conscience with my mother hearing me try and talk, and read out loud to myself for about an hour every day.

I was very self conscience about my speech and did not want to talk to anyone. By practicing reading, my speech did eventually get better but it wasn't overnight. It took a lot of practicing reading to get to that point. Even after reading for a few weeks, I sounded almost normal but I was still self conscience about the way I sounded. I still did not want to talk that much but I did get over that feeling eventually.

Imagine, me not wanting to talk.

Then in the afternoon, I would go to the canal bank that was by our house, with my football. I would practice kicking the ball first. It was kind of embarrassing trying to kick the ball when it only went around 15 yards. Remember I said that the whole right side of my body was weak?, well this was proof that it was. I would kick and kick the football and eventually it would go a little farther. I had this feeling that someone was always watching me, it was almost like I was paranoid about it, I did not want anyone to know that I had suffered a head injury, like it was a sin. Pretty strange, but I think I did not anyone to see me in that condition, I wanted everyone to remember me like I was. Although everyone did not know me, I still thought that they would somehow know the way I used to be.

That's how the accident caused me to feel, like I was inferior although I was far from inferior.

So after reading for an hour and practicing kicking and throwing the football, I would get on my bike and go riding all over, anywhere for about 3 hours. I would not tell my poor mother where I was going because I didn't know, I would just ride. I thought I was recovered, right. I could do as I wanted. It did not matter that I was hard of hearing, all the cars would know that and they would be extra careful when they drove by me, no problem. It did not matter that I wasn't fully recovered mentally. I would not get mad at someone and give them the middle finger and if I did they would know that I had a head injury and not get mad at me. They wouldn't care about what I did to them, I was recovering. I thought I was fully recovered, right.

All this is what I thought.

To put my poor mother through that was very inconsiderate of me, very childish of me and it showed that I was not recovered, no matter what I thought.

After a few weeks it was time for me to go to the junior college where they taught classes for people who were recovering from injuries like I had. There were probably 10 people in my class, people who had different kinds of injuries. The purpose of the classes was to get the students ready to enter the work force again. You would go shopping at a make believe store to see if you would buy the products you needed (they would tell you where you were going or what you were cooking to see if you bought the right things), a typing class (I wish I would have took that class more seriously), to see how you handled things that were new to you, a math class to see how you handled things that you might not know how to do, figure them out. These classes were to see how you reacted to different ways of doing things, things that might have been new to you. These classes were just for you, the teachers new what kind of injury you had and how you would most likely react to doing different tasks. They wanted to see how you reacted to different things, to see how far along you were in your recovery process.

If I would have known the reasons for these type of classes back then when I went to the junior college, I would have given my being there a much more serious approach, but I didn't realize what the reason of my being there was and why I was doing the things I was doing. I would have taken it a lot more seriously, and that is what they look at, how you take those classes.

The same thing happened at the college. I quickly became bored and wanted to leave. I didn't realize the reason I was there. The reason was to become well adjusted to dealing with different people and dealing with doing different tasks. The reason was to get me ready to enter the work force again and succeed at getting back to where I once was.

If I knew then what I know now, things would have been a lot different from me, I guarantee it. I can't state that enough. I would have tried a lot harder at everything I was told to do.

So I started pressuring them to release me from the prison, I thought it was. So they held a formal meeting with the teachers who were responsible for me, me of course, my parents and my social worker who was responsible for getting me back to my original job. He would be in charge of talking to my employer and setting up my return to my previous job.

Everything went well and I was released from the college and my social worker told me what store I was to report to and what time.

Did I just say what store I was to report to and what time I was to report?

I did. That's strange. I thought I would be going back to my store and doing the things I was doing before, seeing the same customers and venders.

Wishful thinking.

I thought I would be going back to my old store and working with my assistant manager during the day. After all, I was the employee who managed to work by myself before my accident, a manager who put up all the stock on Friday working by himself (in between customers), I was the manager who had won company contest for the best appearance and the right amount of inventory and all the other paperwork that the managers had to do, to the store that won an award two out of three years (the only reason I didn't win it my third year is because I did not have my managers smock on when they came to judge the store, we won second place that year, I was only manager for 3 years), I was supposed to get special treatment I thought.

Think again.

Well, it didn't work like that. My father told me that I am only a number to them, maybe a special number, but still a number. I was only an employee to my employer, that's all, no matter what I thought or what I accomplished, period.

My father gave me a lot of good advice back then, when I needed it the most.

So they assigned me to a store that was probably 6 miles away, although the distance was not the problem but the hours were. It was from 3:00 in the afternoon till 11:00 at night. That was a problem. Let me explain.

My mother would drive me there in the afternoon, but she did not drive at night. My father would have to come get me when I got off of work. That would have been a big inconvenience for him, although he never would have told me. He still worked and he went to bed early. He would do anything for his children.

It was still an inconvenience for him AND it would have put me in an awkward position of expecting my father to come pick me up. I still was not released from the doctors care, so to speak, so I could not drive.

So my mother explained this problem to my social worker, and he in turn told my employer about the problem. They in turn changed the stores for me and also changed the times. It would be from 7:00 in the morning until 3:00 in the afternoon.

This was much better for everyone involved, except me and I'll tell you why.

Let me explain to you what happened when I first started working for the company. The store I worked at had this older lady who was the assistant manager. She happened to live at the same apartment complex as my ex- girlfriend at the time. We became social friends because we had something in common, she lived where I went a lot to see my girlfriend. Nothing more than that.

Well about a week after I started working for the company we got a new manager and we became friends. He was a young adult a few years older than I, and after about two weeks he left to go to another store. He asked me if I wanted to go with him to the different store and I said yes. The reason he asked me was because we were both relatively young and he saw what kind of worker I was and we got along really well.

This is not to say that I was superman, but I was simply a good worker.

So I get transferred to the different store with him as manager. After a few weeks I tell him that I want to be an assistant manager so he sends me to the store where they train you to be assistant manager. The lady who trained me was exceptional. After I finished training I was sent to a different store as assistant manager, only after about 6 months. Pretty good I thought.

My friend who sent me to be trained as an assistant manager became supervisor of 7 or 8 stores about this time.

Things were going well for both of us.

Then, after a few months, one of his managers quit and he needed to replace that manager with a new manager.

He came to see me and asked me if I would be interested in the position of manager. It was at a store that was right across the street from the New Orleans Saints training facility and that store was not to far from my house. I said yes.

Things started to accelerate for me as far as my job went.

I went in that store and went to work doing the things I was trained to do, and then some.

We had the first company wide contest to see which manager had the best looking store, as far as appearance went and had all the shelves stocked and the right amount of inventory and all the paperwork you did was graded for mistakes. You would get paid more money for each part of the contest you scored high in. Well my store won out of 150 stores. Not bad for a brand new manager. I forgot to tell you, I was the youngest person at that time to make manager.

Well, fast forward to my going back to work at the store where I worked from 7:00-3:00.

The lady who was the assistant manager at the store where I first started and heard all about it and obviously wasn't a happy camper. She had been assistant manager when I started and still was and I had already been an assistant manager, manager, and won a contest that all the stores where entered in. She was jealous of me, obviously.

What could I do, I did not even know she was jealous of me.

Time went on as usual.

I was making friends at this store, as I always did.

Another year went by and the company had another contest like the first one.

We did not have to do much getting ready because I ran a good store and I, as well as my employer knew it.

This year when they came to judge my store, I was walking out of the "cooler", where the soft drinks, beer, milk, wine etc. is and I did not have my managers "smock" on. The smock was a jacket you put on over your shirt. I always took mine off when I went in the cooler.

The contest was about appearance and having the right amount of inventory not about how you were dressed.

It was a personal thing between the people judging the store (supervisors) and me. They did not like to see anyone be better than they could only hope to be when they were managers.

My store would have won, they told me, but I did not have my uniform on.

We came in second place.

Not bad for a young manager. I was making a name for myself with the company and felt good about myself.

In a few months a manager at one of the stores my friend supervised quit and the store was open for a manager. It was next to a big shopping center and it was situated in a strip shopping center with stores and apartment buildings all around. The store had a big storage area in the back which was good for me as a manager because there was a lot of storage area. My boss, my friend who made me manager, asked me if I wanted to be the manager of that store.

I said yes in a heartbeat because I knew there would be a lot of people coming into the store, and I was right.

I'll get to how this relates to the assistant manager at the store I was at after my accident in a minute.

So I went to my second store happily. I was told who my assistant manager was, it was an older man who was from Ecuador.

The first night I worked I met my first customer. His name was Dutch and we became friends till my accident and then beyond that. He was an older gentleman who came in every day and got coffee and cigarettes. He lived near by in the apartments and I saw him quite regularly.

Meanwhile, my assistant manager and I were getting a good working relationship going. He was very responsible and very dependable and he took a liking to me. Over the course of the next couple of months we became very close and one day he asked me if I went to college. I said yes but didn't graduate. He offered to take me to one of the top colleges in town, Tulane UNIVERSITY and pay the first semester for me. That really knocked me back ten yards.

After going down and looking at the campus with David, I told him that I was flattered but I was happy with what I was doing and that I would have to turn him down.

Can you imagine, someone willing to pay your first semester at one of the top state colleges?

Can you also imagine turning that down?

I've made my share of mistakes in life and that was one of them.

That really meant a whole lot to me that someone would offer to pay for me to go to a year of college.

Life went on at the store for me and David as we continued to meet more customers. I was very outgoing and David was kind of an introvert, quite and very polite.

As I met people, it rubbed off on David since the people would usually come back at night time to get some more things and they would talk to David, who would be working at 3:00 till 11:00. They would usually say that they met me and then that would lead to them talking and David was getting to know more and more people.

Well, the annual contest for the best appearing store with the right amount of stock was coming up. One person I met was a man named Walter who was a painter. Walter offered to paint the whole inside of the store for me for free. I said sure. It would make the whole inside of the store look almost brand new and would give the store a new look, painting over the white walls that were starting to turn yellow.

We started painting one day when he got off of work. It was Friday at around 5:30 and I helped him paint the whole inside of the store. I even had different customers who I knew come in and start washing the windows for me. I had that kind of customers who I called friends and my boss knew that.

Well, I had the shelves stocked with all the right things that people bought, the right amount of inventory, and one thing that I forgot to tell you about was that they looked at your paper work and the least amount of mistakes you had was to your favor. I never had paper work mistakes and I got bonuses for that.

I was simply good at what I did AND liked it.

We had the contest and I don't need to tell you the results, but I will. We won, again.

I'm not bragging but I was good and knew it. I was not arrogant about it but I knew I was good.

The assistant manager who worked at the store were I was stationed at after my accident heard about my store winning the contest AGAIN and this burned her up.

So getting back to the store I was stationed at, this lady, who I thought of as my friend, who I did not know was jealous of me, was supposed to be watching me, observing me as I returned to work, giving the bosses at the company I worked for a report on me.

She was so jealous of me and this was her chance to get me out of her way, to get me fired or demoted so she could move up with the company she worked for; worked for a lot longer than I had. She told them that I was being rude to the customers and that I wasn't doing the cooler, filling it, re-stocking the drinks, beer, and milk, and that I refused to follow orders. That was all the company needed to hear to let me go.

I was one of the highest paid managers and this surely would save the company money.

Like my father said, I was only an employee and nothing more.

They took her word for my performance and fired me. They didn't call my social worker and say I needed more classes at the rehab. Center, they just fired me. Taking another employee's word and not talking to me.

I think that by my being one of the top wage earners among managers and being so young had a lot to do with it.

They fired me, not tell me to return to rehabilitation and then come back, but fired me. The employee who walked to work one day when it flooded and could not drive his car, and not many stores were opening up, but my store did, they fired that manager. The one who won the contest for the best looking and properly stocked store two out of three years, with the least amount of paperwork was fired, the one who thought he would work for the company until he retired, was fired.

All they said was that I wasn't doing my job and this lady who I thought of as a friend was responsible for it.

It was hard for me to believe but it happened and it happened for a reason!

So know I was in uncharted waters. I had received a head injury, got out of the hospital to early by my insistence that I was recovered, by my insistence to my social worker and the teachers at the college I went to for rehabilitation that I was fine. I was like a fish out of water, a person on a rowboat without a paddle.

What should I do.

This ultimately was omen #5, a good omen again. You will see why later on.

Well, the first thing I did was take out the classified ads and start looking for a job.

With no kind of formal training to do anything it was like swimming upstream without a paddle.

Most of the jobs I found were strictly commission. I had a hard time getting a job that paid something above minimum wage.

I did find a job at a shoe store that paid by the hour but that was strictly a menial job. The store was a self serve shoe store where the customers walked around and got the shoes they liked off the shelves by themselves. All you really did was restock the shelves and keep the store looking good.

What got me interested in the job was that the manager told me that they were going to be looking for a manager in a store around 80 miles away. I had good retail experience and thought I might have a chance if I was trained right, which I wasn't.

How do you get trained right for a job at a self-serve shoe store?

There is ways but not at this store.

Doing the paperwork was one thing as was ordering shoes, but I was not trained to do either.

So, I finally quit that job since there was no future for me with that company.

# Chapter Four

One day I'm running some errands with my mother because I still wasn't released from the doctors to drive or social worker officially. We stopped at the bank to make a transaction, and I see this girl who I knew before my accident.

We were friends who liked to talk to each other.

She also had heard about my accident (who didn't) like so many other people.

While my mother is doing her transaction, I start talking to her. She asked me how I'm doing since my accident and I'm a little embarrassed about my accident like it was my fault. I tell her that I'm doing fine and we talk for about ten minutes.

I was kind of embarrassed about my accident?, why it wasn't my fault, but I was.

My mother is waiting for me so we can go.

I gave her my phone number and asked her to call me. I was still self conscience about my speech. I did not want to speak to anyone who I did not know because I thought I sounded different, which I did and one of her roommates might answer the phone.

I think somehow she knew that without my telling her. I said goodbye and my mother and I left.

Two days later on a Friday evening, the phone rang. My mother answered and then said to me that the phone call was for me. It was the girl who worked at the bank!, an old friend who I asked to go skating with me and another friend of mine, also a manager at the company I worked for. We went skating every Thursday night because it was adult night and we had a good time; it was her.

I needed someone to talk to because I never talked to anyone seriously about anything since my accident.

She was a perfect listener and she was interested in what I had to say. It made me feel good that someone was interested in what I had to say.

We talked for well over an hour and I felt good about myself. It was the first time I felt good about myself in a long time.

I kind of felt that I had let myself and people who knew me down, kind of funny.

So I continued looking in the classified's for a job.

Then one day, a friend of mine called, a friend who I had gone to high school with, a friend who also heard about my accident, called me. He was working for an agency finding people jobs.

We talked for a while and he asked me to come to his office and that he would try and find me employment.

His name was Robert Michalik and I went to high school with him and he was an extremely nice person.

By this time I'm driving and so I went to his office to try and get some help.

We talked about old times then he took all kinds of information from me and looked in his files and all that he could come up with was a cook's helper at a Shoney's.

With no training there just was not much out there.

It was not what I was looking for but it was something. I figured that since I was a cook in high school at a local restaurant that I could do the job.

So I went to the restaurant my first day, and was it something. The cook I was helping was a very nervous person. He was always yelling at someone, not just me, but everyone, and he had no patience with anyone.

I figured that this was not for me since my consolers told me to try and be around people who had patience, since I would need patient people to deal with me.

I quit around ten days later, glad to get out of there.

I kept looking in the classified's for a job.

The next job I got was at a young persons clothes shop. It seemed like a good job, I was selling clothes to young people.

There might have been a future with this company, the manager liked me and she knew that I had retail experience, but it just wasn't for me. I needed a job that paid a decent wage, one with a future.

Things were starting to go full force with the girl who worked at the bank, we both liked each other's company. This was a totally different situation for me. I was used to going out with different girls at the same time. I knew that this girl wouldn't go for that and I didn't want that anymore. I don't know if it was my getting older (I was just barely 24) or if I had lost my confidence, but I was starting to settle down. I was getting serious with her and it was time for me to get serious about life in general.

What a change!

# Chapter Five

When I was working at the convenience store, my girlfriend at that particular time, went down to the Post Office to take the test to get hired.

Her step-father worked for the Post Office and had informed her that they would be giving the test to get hired. They only did this whenever they were hiring people, which was not every day.

She asked me to go and take the test with her and I said no because I was happy with my job and that I planned on retiring from the job. It's funny how things work out.

She continued to ask me to go and I finally said yes. I went with her to take the test just to give her moral support.

I was happy with my life the way it was going, not bothering to look to the future.

This would be omen # 6.

Well, they finally wrote her a letter saying that she had scored high enough on the test that if she was still interested to go and take the driving test to get hired.

I was so happy for her. She had finally gotten a good job.

This was about one year before my accident.

She got passed her ninety day probation period where they could fire you for anything, and she was officially hired.

Things looked good for her.

When I had my accident, the Post Office had written me a similar letter also, saying the same thing. I had scored high enough on the test and my name had come up to go and take the driving exam.

Well, my father, who is very intelligent and always looked ahead to see if something would go wrong or could go wrong, what would you do, he wrote the Post Office back informing them that I had been in a car accident and that I was in the hospital recovering, could they please keep me on the list to get hired and could they write back and check again.

Well they wrote back not one more time, but three more times, every time my father replying that I was still in the hospital recovering. When I finally was released from the hospital and finished my rehabilitation I went and took the driving test at the Post Office.

Remember they only write to tell you that you have scored high enough on the test and when there is an opening and when they are giving the driving test, which is not that often.

Before going to take the driving test, I wanted to be sure I was as ready as possible. I went to the State Police station and asked for one of their books that told you what to do when driving, how to be a safe driver.

The book told you a lot of things you probably take for granted. One thing the book said was to stop before you get to the stop sign, do not pass the stop sign up by one foot, but stop BEFORE the stop sign. Pretty simple, but I didn't remember that when I went to take my first driving test to get my license. Another thing they told you was to look in your rearview mirror first then look in your side mirror when switching lanes.

Simple things like that, that you probably take for granted. I wanted to be prepared.

So I go and take the driving test with one other person and I was a little nervous.

We had to take the test not driving a car but a big 5 ton truck. It wasn't a 18 wheeler, but it was a big truck, bigger than a pickup truck. We had to drive in traffic around town. We had to switch lanes on the highway. We had to drive on the interstate. We had to park it and back up. We encountered all kinds of situations and I passed the driving test. Next, I had to go upstairs at the Main Post Office in a big office building and take my physical. This part made me really nervous. Why?, because I was hard of hearing. I lost a lot of my hearing when I had my accident.

I told the doctor that I had to wear a hearing aid and asked him if that mattered.

He said no, as long as I wore my hearing aid.

I was relieved!

So I passed my physical. That was on a Thursday and I was told where to report to tomorrow to start work.

I passed my driving test and my physical and was ready to go to work!

It happened to be the main Post Office in the city where I lived. There where three different zones (zip code sections) at that Post Office that I was told to report to. I was told to report to one zone and the guy I took the driving test with was told to report to another.

I happened to be ahead of him on the seniority list and this will be important as you will see.

And to think, I owed all this to my father for writing the Post Office back and telling them that I had been in a car accident and was in the hospital recovering.

THANK YOU DAD.

So once you go to your zone or zip code, they put you on a ninety day probationary period. They could fire you for anything. If the boss didn't like your personality he could fire you, no questions asked. So of course I was a little nervous.

The first day they had me go out with a training person. He told me how to hold the mail, how to read the addresses etc.. It sounds pretty simple but you have to know how to handle the mail to deliver the mail.

I remember where we went first. It was an apartment building where I first delivered mail. Then it was up and down streets delivering to houses.

It seemed like I would like it.

The first few weeks I was just helping different people. They would get off to go to the doctor or they had something else to do. So I would take different parts of different routes.

Then slowly, I would come in early and case (set up the mail) and deliver the whole route by myself.

I was able to do almost all the routes and I knew which ones I liked and which ones I didn't like.

Just because I came in early and cased the mail and delivered the route, I still had to go and deliver a piece of a different route. You were on the bottom of the totem pole and you just had to do what you were told, no questions asked.

Everything was going fine, my ninetieth day came and I was nervous. I was told to go and deliver this route, not a bad route, in fact I kind of liked it. My boss had not said anything about me passing my probationary period and I was a little nervous.

So I'm out delivering the route, it's about 3:30 and I see my boss come driving up.

My boss was a very friendly person who was always cheerful and always had time to talk to you.

He comes riding up to me and I walk over to his car, nervous as can be.

He rolls his window down and says "hey Russ, when you finish this route go over and help another carrier on a different route". He says that he is going home and that he would see me on Monday.

He starts rolling his window up and I'm just standing there wondering why he hasn't said anything about me passing my ninety days. He could probably tell by the perplexed look on my face that I was wondering if I passed the ninety day period.

I start thinking that I've did all that I was told to do, that I even offered to come in at 4:30 on Saturday mornings to drive the mail to the different Post Offices; they wouldn't have to ask anyone else to do it. Not many people like coming to work at 4:30 in the morning. I'm just thinking.

As he is rolling up his window with me standing there, when the window was half way up he said "you passed your ninety days", smiled, waved goodbye and went home.

I could see him smiling as his window went up and he thought he pulled a good one on me, which he did.

So I'm happy as can be. I finish my route and go help the other carrier and go home. I tell my parents then call the girl who worked at the bank, now I can start calling her "girlfriend". My girlfriend and I go out to eat to celebrate. I forgot where we went but we had a good time, as we always did.

We both enjoyed each other's company.

I was on a roll, I thought.

So life's going pretty good for me.

I'm doing pretty good at work and my relationship with my girlfriend gets better.

Finally after around one year and me doing a lot of thinking, I ask her to marry me. After my accident I was, for the first time, a one girl man, which I'm glad I was and this proved it

She didn't say yes right away, she had to think about it first. She always thinks about EVERY decision she has to make, and I like that, although sometimes I get mad because she takes so long to make a decision and answer me.

Finally after thinking about it for around 10 minutes and she says YES!

I am on cloud nine.

We decide to start saving for the wedding, which was our first financial decision we had to make together.

Then we go and ask a priest who taught me in high school, who's father was friends with my parents (it's a small world) if he would marry us. I'm sure he would say yes.

After talking to him for a few minutes, he says he can't marry us because we haven't been going out long enough (he knows about my accident and wants me to make sure this is what I want, that I'm not just infatuated). He says that he only marries people who have went out at least two years.

It gives you time to get to really know the other person, not just be infatuated with them, he says.

It was O.K. by me, we would just wait since he said he would marry us if we wait another year but my girlfriend got frustrated. She thought we shouldn't have to wait, he has no right telling us to wait and when we can get married!

I tell her that it's alright, that just gives us more time to save for the wedding.

She is really upset but after a few days she see's his point.

So we wait another year while we are saving for the wedding and we start planning the big day.

We set a date after the two years we will have been going out, so he will marry us. We start picking out the songs we want played at the wedding, we start making the list of people to invite. My wife to be starts looking for a wedding dress, I start looking at tuxedos to be worn by the wedding party.

We both start making out the wedding party; I decide who my best man will be, and who will stand in the wedding, who the ushers will be.

It is a big process.

We had three priests marry us and I had to make sure the three priests were available at the same time to marry us. Luckily, they were.

Like I said, Fr. Greg Aymond said the wedding and the other two priest helped. The second priest was also a priest who taught me in high school. This is the priest who accepted me to go to my high school. You had to be accepted to go there and this was the priest who interviewed me to go there.

His name is Fr. Robert Muench and he later became an Archbishop.

The third priest was the priest who was the rector at my parish during my high school years. He gave all the boys who went to this high school a job working at the rectory and gave the seniors a job during the summer cutting the grass and doing other odd jobs.

His name is Ray Hebert and he is a monsignor.

All three of these priest were very instrumental in my teenage years and I will never forget any of them. In fact Fr. Hebert celebrated his 50 years of being a priest and they had a big celebration and dinner for him and Fr. Hebert invited me and my wife to his celebration.

This was a good 15 years after my high school years!

# Chapter Six

I picked as my best man a friend who I had met while I was in high school. His name is Louis Colmenares. He is an artist who makes and does everything and anything. He paints, makes jewelry, makes furniture, makes costumes, anything. If you ask him to do something for you, he will, maybe not right away but he will do it. He can do anything.

One time he told me that the only thing he couldn't do was play the piano and I'm sure he will do that to one day. Of course he was only joking.

One year for Halloween he made a dragon costume that shot smoke out of its mouth, its eyes lit up and it was BIG.

I wore it to seven costume contests and we won seven contests easily, no one came close.

We won money, bar tabs, plane trips, weekend at hotels, you name it. This guy is an ARTIST and he is great at what he does.

To me, that's what an artist is, a person who does anything.

We hung out together in high school a lot and we just became close.

Like I said though, he is an artist, and those people are different.

The wedding day is getting close and I picked him to be my best man, he say's yes months before. I try calling him and even going to his house a few times and I can't get in touch with him. I start to worry. My wife starts to worry, with that look like "I told you not to ask him to be your best man".

What happened to Louis? Did he get arrested or get shot. I'm really worried about him. So out of desperation I ask another friend who is standing in the wedding to be my best man, his name is Mitch Foto. I tell him what happened and he understands so he says he will be my best man. Then on the day of the wedding, Louis shows up thinking he will be the best man and I tell him the situation I was in. Luckily for me he understood and he just stood in the wedding.

He just said he went out of the state for a while on a vacation.

Artist have a different type of personality but he is a good friend.

So that morning my sister's boyfriend take me and my father out to breakfast, just the three of us.

When my sister and he came to see me in the hospital, I remember calling him Steve. His name is Michael and Steve was the name of my sisters first husband. That was the first time I met him and I'm sure I made a good first impression on him (right Russ).

On March 14 we tied the knot.

My wife to be was perfectly calm; I on the other hand was a little nervous about anything that could go wrong, anything that would mess things up.

The wedding was in the afternoon. It was a good day, no rain and the wedding went off just fine. After the wedding ceremony we went to the reception and had a blast.

Along with my sister and her to-be husband, my aunt, my father's sister and my second cousin, my father's first cousin, came in to town for the wedding. Also, with my wife's parents came a few of her sister's and brother-in-laws and nephews and nieces and cousins. My wife comes from a very big family.

With all of my friends and my wife's parents and friends and relatives, and my parents friends there, it was a good time.

It was good seeing so many of my friends there and every one having a good time.

When we went to leave the reception, we saw that Louis, the artist, had written all over my car with SHOE POLISH!, we thought is was shaving cream, we thought nothing of it. While we were on our honeymoon we went through a car wash and tried to get the (supposed shaving cream off). It was not coming off. We had to compound the whole car to get the shoe polish off, and that's after going threw the car wash numerous times trying to get it off! We laugh about it now but it was not a laughing matter then. Louis had gotten into our suitcases also and managed to put rice in the locked suitcases. How he managed that I do not no since they were locked.

When we left the reception, we stopped at a restaurant that was near by to use the bathroom, and the restaurant we stopped at was the restaurant I had gone to so many times when I used to go out with different people on the weekends.

Almost everyone of my friends from the reception was there!

We used the bathroom, told them goodbye and left.

Later on we both said we should have stayed at the restaurant with all of my friends. We both regret not staying but we had reservations that we had to get too.

So we went to Disney World but when we arrived there, I forgot all of my cash at home! I told you I was a little nervous. I had taken cash out of the bank to use on our honeymoon and put it in the pocket of my jacket that I wore after the reception. For some strange reason I left the jacket with my mother and just wore a shirt when we left. The money was in the pocket of that jacket!

We just used the cash I had in my wallet and the cash my wife had in her purse and we charged the rest.

Luckily, we both had charge cards or our marriage would have started out on the wrong foot, so to speak.

We went to Disney World and had a great time!

We had a great time driving to Florida and back from Disney World and when we arrived back home we were still on a high.

When I went back to work, I got off at around 3:30 and my wife would come home at 5:00. She would prepare a big meal every day! A big three or four course meal after working all day.

It didn't dawn on me to start getting dinner prepared but I was new at getting married, and did not know what to do, if you will.

She would make sure that we did not eat fast food every day. That's the kind of person she is.

We lived in a small 1 bedroom apartment for about a year. It was a nice apartment but very small and we eventually grew out of it.

One day my wife say's out of the blue "when are we going to start looking for a house".

Well, I knew we would buy a house ONE day but I never thought about it until she said that. My wife always thinks ahead, just like my father does.

My wife's sister's sister-in-law (that's a hard one to understand) worked for a real estate company and she got an agent to show us some houses. I guess we looked at six houses and we finally settled on one that we liked. It was a small starter house for us. It was a nice three bedroom house with a big two car garage in the back and behind that the owner had built an office with a telephone, A.C. and electricity. It was a really nice house in a nice neighborhood.

So we put a bid in and it was accepted. We were doing good for ourselves. We move in and after about a year my wife met a divorced lady who lived across the street and she became one of my wife's best friends. She would come over when my wife was doing garden work and help her and they would just talk about anything. She was an older lady who would give my wife advice on a lot of different things. My wife would always take her to the store, although she drove and had a car, my wife just likes to help people.

She was almost like my wife's soul mate. She was that special.

Then one day out of the blue, my wife say's "when are we going to have a baby". There she goes again, she thinks ahead. I knew we would have a baby one day, I just never thought about it. I said that's a good idea. My wife always thinks ahead and I guess I don't.

So we try and have a baby and we are successful right away. We are both so happy. My wife finds out she has to have a "C" section. It's no big deal to me since I'm a man but to her she say's she will miss the labor pains. I guess it's a girl thing, but I thought that would be good, right!

Wrong!

It's Sunday night around 9:30 and her baby shower was that afternoon and she is looking at all the baby gifts she received in the baby room we had set up, and I'm in the living room watching the movie "Arthur".

I think that is the funniest movie I have seen I love that movie.

She calls me in the baby's room and says we should go to the hospital, she thinks her water broke. So we take the bag we prepared with all of the essentials and go to the hospital. The doctor says that her water bag has indeed broke and that she would indeed have the baby that night. Great I thought! Why?, because the next day was my birthday. I thought she would be born on my birthday!

Let me tell you why this is important to me.

When I was in high school a good friend of mine that I met at high school, that also stood in the wedding, his name is Darren Vicknair, well his birthday was the same day as mine. We remain friends and talk once in a while on the phone. We always invite him and his family to our Christmas party that we have every year.

He was married during my stay at the hospital, good timing for me, right. Well one of his children was born on his birthday which happens to be my birthday!

Well my wife having a "C" section guarantees that the baby would be born on my birthday which is my friends birthday and his child's birthday. I thought that would be great!

I asked the doctor if he could wait until 12:01 and deliver the baby. For some strange reason, the doctor said no.

The doctor who delivered my first child couldn't and wouldn't wait 25 minutes!

She was born at 11:35 at night, 25 minutes before my birthday!

Well, so much for the thought of having a special day. My daughter has her own birthday, which she should.

Anyway, you know we had a daughter and she was and still is precious, although she is growing up and has an opinion on everything, sort of like me.

My wife and I were so happy.

We came home from the hospital and my wife was and still is, very patient with her. She is a teenager now and this really does put you through the test.

Almost a year after my daughter was born, I'm reading the paper and I read this story about a family that lives in a trailer with a little girl. It's around Christmas time and the little girl would run around the trailer yelling that Santa Claus is coming. Well there was a fire one day and the trailer was destroyed the little girl died in the fire.

This story touched me like I'm sure it would most people, especially new parents.

So I decide to start a business with "The National Missing Children Foundation". This is a little candy or mint machine you put in businesses with pictures of children that were kidnaped, or ran away. There was two pictures of a child with information about the child and a 800 phone number to call if you can help. Every month I would change the pictures and put pictures of a different child on the machines. Every month I would send the company a check out of the money I collected from the machines.

The company found a lot of the kids and this was just my way of helping children. I felt I needed to help children out in some way.

We had this business for around three years and finally sold it for the same amount that we had bought it for.

It wasn't a bad investment but it was time consuming going to the different locations every week and re-filling the machines with mints.

All in all we raised our daughter to have good morals and she is very bright, in fact she got straight A's in grammar school and she has gotten A's and B's in her first two years of high school.

One day when my wife and I got in an argument, I went outside and wrote a poem for my daughter. I've always wrote poetry and this poem I had calliogragraphed and put her picture on it at about the age she was when I wrote it. I then had it framed.

I don't know why I wrote a poem about my daughter but the argument must have had something to do with her.

I had the poem published I will give it to her when she get's married and has children of her own.

The poem is published in a book of poems that I bought for her.

Well, my wife does it again. She say's "why don't we have another baby". She say's that our daughter will need a sibling to play with and talk to sometimes. My response is that we have one very smart daughter who we can give anything within reason to. Why rock the boat.

We go back and forth and I finally see her side of the equation, if you will.

Our daughter will need a sibling to play with and talk to (and push around).

So we decide to try and have another child.

We are successful again and my wife has to have another "C" section and this time the baby is born on the first day of the month I was born in! Not bad. All three of us are born in February and my wife is born in November.

So now my daughter is four years old with her baby brother. My daughter met some twins in pre-k and has been friends all through grammar school and in grammar school she also made another friend. All these friends of hers are straight A students with good morals. She has made good friends and we are very proud of her.

One of the many things my daughter did in grammar school that we were happy about was do a dance with some boys and girls from her class to the theme song of the T.V. series Friends.

She along with nine of her friends, five girls and five boys total, made up a dance that they danced to during the song. Their dance was something "N/Sync might have done, everyone doing the same thing. At the end they all had umbrellas that they opened up that said "friends" in capital letters, one letter per umbrella. It was very good performance that we and all the other parents are proud of.

Another thing we did while my daughter was in grammar school was start another home based business. This one was a vending machine business.

We bought machines that sold soft drinks, any kind, Coke, Pepsi etc. juices and snacks, all built into one machine. You could also take the snack machine off and have the juices and snacks in two different locations if you wanted. You could charge a different price for everything in the machine. The machine was totally mechanical except the condenser to keep the soft drinks and juices cold so it used LESS electricity. It was also very compact and "sleek" looking so we had no problem getting locations for the machines, although the company helped you get the locations. They did a lot for their customers, which we were.

After we set up the first location, people would see the machines and call us, (we had our company name and the phone # on a business card taped to the machine), and they would ask us if we could put one of the machines in their business.

We had this business three years and after a while it got to be too much for my wife to do, she was running to the different locations refilling them. We had some locations on the second floor and for her to carry the soft drinks and juices up two flights of stairs was hard work for a lady and when we went on vacation we had to find someone we trusted to fill the machines for us. Some of the locations had to be filled twice a week.

Plus our daughter was in pre-k now and our son had to be taken care of when my wife went to re-fill the machines, it just got to be too much. My wife wanted to raise our children and not have a nursery do that.

The reason it was hard to find someone was because when you opened the machines to re-fill them, the money was there in one big tray. It wasn't locked with the money going to a separate location. So you had to find someone you trusted to take the money out of the machines.

We couldn't always find someone to fill the machines for us and some machines would stay empty for a week or so.

We finally sold the machines around three years later. We had to get a business broker to sell them and we also got back our initial investment.

Not bad, we got back our investment after running both businesses for around three years and selling them.

Around this time, we had to start looking for a high school for my daughter. We looked at three and then my daughter picked one of the three. She picked one that had a very good reputation and that we liked. All three were good schools so she couldn't go wrong with the pick she made.

It was a Catholic high school that we are pleased with.

She's doing fine in that school, getting A's and B's and she is coming into her own.

What I mean is that in grammar school she followed the crowd, a very good crowd, but she still followed the crowd. Now she makes decisions based on what she wants to do, which every parent wants the children to do. She went off and made new friends which made both of us SAD but that was her decision and we stand behind her for that. We thought her friends from grammar school would be friends for life.

Some of the friends she made in grammar school was Sarah, Megan, and Nicole and all three are very special to me simply because they were my daughters first friends and they are good young ladies.

My son has also made friends but he goes to a smaller school. He has made some good friends too. Joseph, Andrew, Joey, and Jeremy are some of the friends he has made and they too are good kids who have good morals.

His school goes from grammar school through high school but it still is a very a small school. They put a lot of emphasis on their academics.

He already wants to be an NBA player and practices almost every day.

He knows all the good players and what teams are doing good. One of his favorite players is Kobe Bryant. My son has good taste when it comes to basketball players.

He is very good at basketball but still young. I can't wait for him to play at his school, he'll probably play junior varsity at first but you never know. He is also a very bright kid like his sister and they both have very good morals.

My son already told me when he gets to the N.B.A. he is going to buy me a brand new Corvette and his mother a brand new Nissan Mirano. That would be nice. He's already thinking ahead and wants to reward us.

They are both growing up just fine and that makes my wife and I very happy.

When he was about one year old I also wrote a poem for him and had his picture when he was about one year old put at the bottom and then had it caligriographed. I also had his poem published and will give the poem and book that published it to him when he get's married.

I'm very proud of my son and daughter, and also of my wife. I haven't said too much about my wife because words can't explain how good of a person she is. That comes from my heart. She is the best wife a man can have AND she is a great mother to our children.

What more can you ask for?

# Chapter Seven

When we started our second home based business we also had to start looking for a bigger house since we were out growing our first house and we needed a place to store the cases and cases of soft drinks and juices and candy, potato chips, and snacks that we were buying. The candy we put in the spare bedroom to keep the chocolate from melting but having it within reach of us was very tempting to both of us and sometimes we depleted some of the candy and cookies that we kept in the house.

We looked and looked for a different house for about a year and a half with no luck.

We would find houses that were fine for us and then we would look at how the house would be with an in-law house added on. We would need a house with a pretty big lot to add an in-law house simply because we did not want to build a little room with a bathroom for my parents.

So we kept on looking.

One day I'm delivering mail to this house three blocks away from our house and when I go walking up to the house the owner of the house has his door open and is working on the stairs. He see's me and comes walking over to me to get his mail. I give it to him and say "how are you", we do a little small talk and then I say and that my wife and I have seen the floor plan of his house and like it. I ask him if he would be interested in selling his house. He replies that his wife has very bad arthritus and they were thinking about selling it.

I find a house that doesn't have a for sale sign in front, my wife and I have already seen the floor plan and like it, the owner is in no hurry to sell so we can sell our house without rushing and the neighborhood is good, right by our present house! What more can I ask for?

That was omen # 7.

So when I leave the house and finish the block with my mail, I call my wife and tell her that I found a house we both like and that we should go see it. We make an appointment for the next night to go over and see the house. Like I said we saw the floor plan and approved of it. The next night we go over and look at the house. The owner and his wife take us on a tour of the house and like I said, we know the floor plan and already approve of it. In one of the upstairs bedrooms, he has it set up to lift weights. He has mirrors on the walls and door. I think that the mirrors have to come down when my son or daughter moves in there. The middle room was a kind of loft that has a T.V. and sofa in it. I think we could close the room by putting a wall up in the hall way and closing the part that comes up by the stairs. The master bedroom is huge and like I said we already approved of it. All in all, we both like the house.

So his wife tells us that they would ask between a certain price range. We say, fine, we'll give you so much for the house and they accept it.

We shook hands and that was it!

So we get a real state agent to list our house for us. We get an offer about three or four weeks later. We counter that offer and they accept! We are on our way, we are moving up. We are getting a bigger house in a nice neighborhood.

We are both very excited!

So all in all, the closing on both houses goes pretty good.

We move in on fathers day weekend. We start making changes to the house, making it our house. We had new kitchen counter tops put in, we had a breaker box replace the fuse box that was out dated, we had new double-panned windows with argon gas installed, we had a new garage door put on the garage and we had a sun room built in the back that had pilings under ground, electricity, a A.C. and a phone. We thought we were moving up, which we were.

We were still living within our means.

We were still looking for another house or we were trying to decide whether to add on to this house for my parents.

It was always something we had to think about, but we weren't complaining about the situation.

We had contractors come over to the house and give us estimates to build an in-law house on top of the garage. We even thought of installing an elevator for my parents to get up and down from the second floor; we would have built it over the garage and they would have to get used to going up and down the stairs every day; they lived in a one story house and they were both getting up in age.

So all good things come to an end.

I'll tell you about what I mean and try and keep it short.

There is this very outdated house next to ours and the family decides to move.

A man, lady and three kids bought the house next to us and they were very different, the husband, wife and three kids. They were sheltered in an apartment up until now, no big deal. For some strange reason, they did not like us, even though I brought them a pizza the day they moved in, even though I offered him a weed eater since he was a grass cutter; they just did not like us, jealous of me I guess but why?

We were still looking for a house with an in- law house since we decided not to add on to our house when our agent showed us a single house that we both fell in love with. It was in a nicer neighborhood and it was the perfect house for us.

So we put a bid in on it and they accepted it. They were in no hurry to move because they were building a new house and it would not be ready for a few months. We had not sold our house yet and that gave us time to sell it.

It seems like we went through this with our other house.

Anyway, they wanted to go ahead with the closing so we decided to rent the house to them until we sold our house. So we rented it back to them until we sold our house, and until we sold our house they were paying our house note. It worked out good for both of our families.

We finally sold our house a few months later and you would not believe what we went through. The couple that bought it was not even married yet. They were going to get married in a few months but you could tell they were new to buying a house as they should be and really did not know what to do. Their agent waited until after the ten day inspection period and told us they wanted a video inspection of the sewer pipes. We just had the pipes replaced ten months earlier and we didn't see a problem with that, although our agent did not agree with us, but we said let the have an inspection. They came and ran a video and found out that the water was not draining right from the pipes, at the right angle. They were not angled right. So my wife called the plumber who did it and told him the problem, that the pipes HE replaced were not at the right angle, so he had people out there at 6:00 A.M. the next morning re-hanging all the sewer pipes, making them right.

He was saving his reputation!

While they were running the video inspection they found a crack between the house and the sidewalk. We could either fix it or have the people buying the house fix it and pay them for the labor cost. They decided they wanted us to have it fixed, which was no problem. We had it fixed just because we wanted to move very badly, because the neighbors we had, the situation warranted us moving. It got so bad with the neighbor that we would have taken 10,000 LESS just to move away, but anyway that's water under the bridge. Then there was a water stain on the ceiling and they thought the stain was from water leaking from the tub directly above it. We paid to have a plumber come out and check the tub to see if there was a leak. He checked the tub and told us there was no leak from the tub upstairs, that the stain was probably from years ago. That wasn't good enough for them, they wanted their plumber to check it out. Fine, they would pay for it, so what did it matter. Their plumber came out, who just happened to be related to them and he was spraying water from the shower head into the hot and cold faucets where the water came out, still nothing. Guess what he did? He told my wife to go downstairs and look at the ceiling and see if there is any water coming out. He couldn't be wrong, so he put some water where he was supposed to find some water and called her back up and said he found the leak. Pretty sneaky. All this happened because we agreed to let them inspect the house after the ten day inspection period. Lesson learned, always listen to your agent when buying or selling a house.

We wanted to leave the neighborhood and my parents were getting old but we couldn't find a house that had an in-law house attached to it.

It worked out for the best.

# Chapter Eight

---

We bought the house and we fell in love with it. My parents came over to see it and my father and mother liked it also.

A few months before, my father had been diagnosed with Alzheimer's disease and it was progressively getting worse. My mother was taking care of him and she would call us up whenever she and my father went some where and my father decided not to get out of the car. We, if I was home, would go to where ever they were, which was usually the drug store and wait with my father until my mother got what she needed, which was usually medicine. She was a light sleeper and she would hear when my father would get up in the middle of the night. He would tell her that he was going to work.

My father had retired from work years ago. If my mother would not have been a light sleeper my father would have drove somewhere and besides getting lost, might have hit and injured someone and possibly killed them!

So she took care of him as long as she could AND she took exceptional care of my father. Then it was decided by my mother and me, and my sister as well as my father's doctor that it was time for my father to go to in an assisted living center.

My mother had done all that she was capable of doing for my father.

We, my mother, myself and my wife looked at all the places around our home and we decided to put him in a very nice and new assisted living center not to far from our house.

My mother and wife put the clothes that he would need, a brand new T.V. for him to watch and whatever else he would need, like toothpaste and a toothbrush and shampoo in a bag and brought it over there one day when someone came to stay with my father at home.

My father loved baseball and all the old players like Joe D'Maggio, Phill Rizzuto, Babe Ruth etc.. His favorite player of all time was Joe D'Maggio. He had seen Babe Ruth play also and he could never forgive New York for selling the Dodgers to California years ago.

The only thing left was getting my father over there. He would never go willingly.

A week before he went in, our friend Bernice Yuratich, a professional photographer, who we know because her son and my son are friends at the same school, omen # 8, took pictures of my family as well as my parents with their grand kids. We had great pictures of everyone, especially my father with his granddaughter and his grandson as well as me with both of my parents as well as my wife with both of my parents. They all turned out so good, it's almost unbelievable.

Bernice took a picture of my wife, daughter, son and me that turned out just remarkable.

If we would have waited one more week, my father would not have had the frame of mind to take the pictures.

It's funny how things work out.

That was omen # 9.

So anyway, I said I would bring him myself on a Sunday.

The doctor said that it would be better if just someone would bring him, that my mother should stay home because it would just confuse him if his caretaker, which was my mother, would leave him there alone.

Everything that he needed was already over there, his toothbrush, clothes etc.

My mother even took some family pictures of my family with his grand kids and my sister with her family as well as a picture of his sister over to the assisted living center and hung them up.

So everything was ready for my father to fit in, so to speak.

My wife, who loved my father like her own father, said she wanted to go with me to give me support. I knew it was because she loved my father deeply and wanted to be with him. I said no, that just I would take him but we talked and I decided to let my wife come also, because my father loved her like his own daughter. Also it made it easier for me.

My wife as well as my mother are much stronger people than I am.

So we both took my father there on a Sunday. We told him that we were just taking a ride because he would never agree to go to an assisted living center. We told him that his doctor said he wanted to do some test on him at the assisted living center and that he would have to stay there for the night.

That was very hard for me, to lie to my father, who had never lied to me and had been a good father to me my whole life.

So my wife and I took my father for a ride first, mostly me just talking to him. I told him that all my years growing up he and my mother had given up so much for me and that they had always given me the best and that I truly did appreciate it, now it was time for me to take care of him.

I don't think he truly understood what I meant because he said nothing in reply, or maybe he did understand, I will never know.
Then we started going toward the center where he would stay at.
We drove up and we got out the car and went inside. We told them who we were and they told us they were expecting us (they knew we would be bringing my father there that afternoon) and that his room was right there, pointing right there next to the entrance.
We took my father inside his room and told him that he would be staying there that night. He asked us if he would be staying by himself and I said that I had to go to work in the morning and that my wife had to take care of our children, and that yes, he would have to stay there by himself.
We showed him his bed and the pictures that mom had brought over; my wife and I and his grandchildren along with my sister, her husband and their teenager, and his sister. He liked the pictures and then we walked around. We showed him where he would be eating at and we met some other people who were staying there, trying to help him fit in.
My father likes to be by himself except for his family and grandchildren and doesn't like to socialize that much. One day way before he was diagnosed with Alzheimer's disease I saw him standing outside of our house talking to Mr. Roberts, a neighbor of ours that we grew up with, laughing and talking about the

war, World War II, which my father was an interrogator in. He was a five language interrogator and he knew that his generation changed the way Americans live today, that his generation changed American history for the better.

He was very proud of his generation, and rightly so.

It made me feel so good to see and hear my father sharing stories and laughing with Mr. Roberts.

That isn't to say that my father did not excel. He was a superintendent on the river and he did his job well AND he liked what he did.

He used to take the family down to the river when we were younger and show us the ships that would come to the port of New Orleans, almost every week. He would always bring something home that the captains of the ships from all over the world would give him. Captains from Japan, (my father could not stand the Japanese because of World War II), Russia, France (the same thing as the Japanese) Germany just to name a few.

Getting back to my father at the assisted living center, we went outside to the courtyard and sat down and just talked for a long time.

I mostly reminisced with him. My wife talked to him also but mostly let me do the talking.

So finally after a couple of hours, we left him there by himself. It was getting close to dinner time and we told him that he would be eating in a few minutes.

My wife and I drove home almost in silence but one thing she said that I will always remember is "Russ, I thought you said the right things especially about you taking care of him". For my wife to say that to me meant a lot. My wife only say's things that are true and that she means. It made me feel so good to hear that but never the less, it did not make me feel good that my father was there.

So we go back to see my mother, who had my daughter stay with her, kind of like to give her moral support, and she asked us how it went. We said fine, which was a lie. It didn't go fine, but it was something that had to be done.

My mother would go there every day and stay with him, making sure they gave him the right food to eat. They had a list of the food he could eat and what he couldn't eat, but it was like not giving them a list at all. It was like they couldn't read! It seemed like they would give him whatever they were giving everyone else!

My mother would see them giving him food he shouldn't eat and not giving him his medicine at the proper times. She would tell them that he could not eat that food, but it was like not telling anyone at all. So it was good that my mother was there everyday, in effect caring for him.

When my mother was there she took better care of my father then they did. SHE fed him the food that he could eat since they continued to feed him food he couldn't when they had a paper that said what he could not. My mother was staying there until 4:00 pm and my father was given better care when she was there.

My wife would stop by there when she got off of work and he was always glad to see her. When I got off of work I would go there and see him. With Alzheimer's, there is a period that starts at around 3:00 or 4:00 in the afternoon and it is called "the sundown time". This is an especially hard time for them because they quickly become agitated and confused. I would walk around with him and talk to him. One day while I was there and walking and talking to him, he said "I love you Russ". That meant a lot to me because it showed me that he knew what was going on with him and at that moment he was all right, and that he meant it. My father never said that he loved me but I just knew it.

He meant what he said.

Then he went back into the sundown time, it was like he came out of it for a few minutes then went back to it, no choice of his own.

My mother called me one night at around 6:30 and said that Dad had slipped broken his hip and had to go to the hospital, would I come get her and take her to the hospital. There was no need for an answer, I definitely would. I went and picked up my mother and we went to the hospital.

When my mother had called, I was preparing food for a priest friend of ours that would be eating with us the next night.

When we arrived at the hospital, he had already been transported there, the doctor came and talked to us. He said that they found my father sitting on the floor at the assisted living center, that he had fell and broke his hip. The doctor explained that you break your hip first AND then fall, just the opposite of what people think, you fall, and break your hip.

The nurses didn't know how long he was sitting on the floor.

He had to go to the hospital and the doctors would operate on him that night if we chose that.

We stayed all night and the nurse told my mother that the anesthesia would progress the Alzheimer's disease. Well my mother, the thoughtful person she is, asked the doctor this question, would it progress the disease. The doctor confirmed it.

My father came out of the surgery fine, the surgery went well. He was more relaxed and at peace, which was a blessing in disguise. I'll explain.

My father was like a model patient, never complaining, never yelling, just very peaceful.

While he stayed at the hospital a few days my mother told her dentist, who is a Christian person and knows just about everyone who does everything, that my father had broken his hip and that he had to go to the hospital. He couldn't go back to the assisted living center because they wouldn't have the people there who were trained to care for a person who couldn't walk. He would have to leave and go to another center, probably a nursing home. Could he possibly help her out.

There was a nursing home directly behind the hospital that he had been in for the surgery. A silent blessing in disguise.

My mother had already inquired about putting my father there but they had a long waiting list to get in. Chances are he wouldn't have gotten in.

The dentist told my mother not to worry about it, he would get my father in there.

How would he, my mother thought?

My mother and my father had been patients of Dr. Briggs years before he had been diagnosed with Alzheimer's.

Sure enough, Dr. Briggs got my father into that nursing home.

He knew the administrator of the nursing home and he was able to get my father in there without waiting. He would go there once a week to clean the patients teeth so they knew and liked him.

That meant that my father wouldn't have to go to the nursing home that was ten miles away in the city.

That was omen # 9.

My mother was there every day just like at the assisted living center. She took care of my father better than the help that was there. She fed him; again, they had a list of what he could eat and what he couldn't and again they continued to give my mother the wrong food to feed him because my mother was feeding him breakfast and lunch. She would let them feed him dinner because it would start getting dark outside and she wanted to get home, not being a nighttime driver.

It must be an occupational hazard to read the patients menu, of what they can't eat because this happened at the assisted living center also.

The workers refused to read what the patients were allowed to eat and what they weren't allowed to eat.

Everyday my mother fed my father breakfast and lunch and brushed his teeth. My wife would stop by on her way home from work before she had to pick up our children from school. Every day I would stop by when I got off work and see him before I went home.

I'll never forget this; on July 4$^{th}$ weekend we went there on a Sunday and celebrated the 4$^{th}$ of July with him. We brought sandwiches and cake and drink to him and we sat outside and ate and talked. Before we went outside to eat, since it was a nice day, my father had a red white and blue styro-phone hat hanging on the wall for the 4$^{th}$ of July.

Well my son, spur of the moment, took the hat off the wall, put it on and pointed to my father saying "we want you", like they did during the draft of WWII.

Were my son learns about these things, like "uncle Sam pointing" at the camera, I do not know, but like I said, my son is very smart like his sister.

My father thought that was funny and laughed and laughed. He thought that was so funny; for that one minute, my father came out of his disease and he knew what my son was doing.

And that day was the last time my father laughed AND my son made him laugh.

I'm very proud of my son for doing that.

That was omen # 10.

My father, when he was well, loved his grandchildren, not only our children but my sisters son also, and I am so proud of my son for making him laugh.

Sometimes I ask my son who made his grandfather laugh the last time and he says he did.

# Chapter Nine

---

The hospital is being sold to another hospital in a matter of weeks. My father did well for about three weeks. Then my mother noticed he was having trouble breathing, he was heaving. She told the nurse and the nurse said, get this, that he was constipated. Constipated! My mother told his doctor and his doctor, who would go to the nursing home on Saturday, said he would do an x-ray and see what the problem was.

So it's a good thing my mother was on top of things or they would have left him like that, constipated like the nurse said!

The doctor ordered an x-ray and my mother received a call on the following Monday informing her that my father had advanced pneumonia. The doctor said there wasn't really anything they could do for him.

Once the doctor told my mother that, it was like my father heard him say that he had advanced pneumonia, he went down hill from that moment. My father wouldn't eat and didn't eat. He didn't recognize my mother, who was with him every day, me, my wife or his grandchildren. He stopped talking, although he wasn't talking much, he would say one or two words, but no more.

That was on Monday.

On Friday I tell my friend at work, Robert McGarry, what's going on with my father, keeping him informed about the situation, and he almost insisted that I don't come to work the next day, that my family needs me to be there. We go back and forth on whether I should come to work tomorrow or not and I finally agree with him that I should be with my family at the hospital.

That same Friday, I get a call at work and it's my wife. I'm out on the street already and she say's that my father doesn't look so good; I should go to the hospital.

She went to the hospital every day before she went to work so she kept me informed on my father's condition along with my mother, who would call me in the afternoon.

That's all I needed to hear. I bring my mail back to the station, tell the station manager that I have to go to the hospital, they know what's going on with my father, and I go to the hospital. My mother is there by herself with my father when I walk in.

I go give my mother a hug and give my father a kiss. He is sleeping and at this time and only wakes up for about three minutes every hour or so. I don't remember if I or my mother called my sister, but she was told my father wasn't doing good at all, she should come home as soon as possible. My sister and her family lives in New Jersey and she got a flight to New Orleans right away and was with us that afternoon.

The whole time we're waiting for my sister to arrive, I'm praying that my father hangs on until my sister get here. He loved his daughter immensely and I wanted my sister to see her father alive one last time.

My sister walked in to the hospital room at around three in the afternoon. My mother and I inform her as to how my father is doing, or not doing. My father's doctor comes in and my sister and mother talk to him, I'm there too, but not really listening to them, although I do catch some of what is being said.

I remember my mother told me way before that if my father goes into a vegetive state, that she doesn't want to put a feeding tube in him. I said that was her decision and that whatever she decides, I will stand besides her.

I hear her telling the doctor that she doesn't want a feeding tube put in him, and I walk over to the conversation. I hear the doctor telling my mother and sister that they would give my father an I-V with liquid so he wouldn't dehydrate. Mt father stopped eating by himself (somebody was feeding him) a long time ago.

The doctor said that my father was not in any type of pain and that he seemed very peaceful and relaxed.

My first wish came true in that my sister was able to see her father one last time.

That night, Friday, I slept at the hospital with my father. It was kind of a quiet night as far as things go with my father. Around two in the morning the nurses come in to check on his I-V and I wake up; they tell me that they were just checking on his I-V and that I can go back to sleep.

My mother and sister come over in the morning, around 7:00 and then my wife comes over a little while later with my children. We all start talking about whether Hospice should come in or not.

This is where it gets kind of "hectic".

The hospital is being sold to another hospital in a matter of weeks and this is a very important. We are told that Hospice can not come to this hospital since it is being sold, that in order for Hospice to have my father as a patient we would have to transfer my father to a different hospital about twenty miles away. We all agree that this is out of the question, we are not transferring my father anywhere.

We are on the phone around three total hours talking to different people. We still haven't decided what to do.

My mother and sister say they are hungry and ask me if it is all right if they go downstairs to the cafeteria and get something to eat. I said that was O.K. and my wife says she is going to go home and take a shower and come back and spend the night with my father.

I say that we both can stay and she says that she wants to stay with him by herself. I say that's O.K. and she leaves with my daughter and son, but before my wife leaves, she tells my children to tell there grandfather goodbye. My son gives my father a kiss goodbye and then my daughter bends down and gives her grandfather a kiss goodbye. It looked like she knew this would be the last time she saw her grandfather alive, and I think subconscientiously, she knew that.

She gave him a very special "I love you" kind of kiss.

My wife gives her father-in-law a kiss goodbye and tells my father that she will be back in a little while, like she knew my father could hear her. For all I know, my father did hear my wife because they had such a remarkable, caring, and bonding for each other.

My mother and sister go downstairs to get something to eat.

It's around six o'clock in the evening and I'm alone with my father. I sit down to read the paper. My father has his eyes closed and I am looking at him just thinking about life, and how it appears to be so unfair sometimes, but then I remember all the good things my father had done for me during my lifetime and I think I made out alright but my children will miss out on all of my fathers love and good will. My mother and my father were always there whenever my children did ANYTHING in school; how I wanted my father to see my daughter graduate from high school, he would have cried proud tears. Then I realize that I'm being selfish and that my father deserves to go to heaven and be with his parents.

I start reading the paper and about a half hour later my father starts breathing really fast and loud and opens his eyes real wide.

I walk over to my father and say"what's wrong dad". He starts looking through the ceiling, not at the ceiling but through it and he's turning his head back and forth, not hearing a word I'm saying.

What he's looking at?

He's looking at JESUS and his mother and father and they are calling him to come join them. I feel so proud of what my father had accomplished and at the same time, sad. About five nurses come rushing in; there was a monitor connected to him and to the front desk where they could keep up on any changes that would happen to my father, like this one. As they rush in, they tell me to leave the room.

I have no intention of leaving the room.

I take my cell phone out of my pocket and called my mother and sister to tell them that they better get back but I can't get through to them. Luckily they were in the elevator coming up at the time I called them. I called my wife and told her that she should get over here right away.

Somehow my wife knew what was going on; she calls her good friend Dianne McBride and asks her if she could come over to our house and stay with the children while she goes to the hospital. They (Dianne and her husband) come over right away, dressed as if they were getting ready to go out, which they were, and stay with our children, and my wife rushes over.

My wife did not want to take our children to the hospital at that time.

My wife is rushing to the hospital and she is almost there when all of a sudden she slows down as if she knew what happened to my father, and she thinks "I told Russ's father goodbye already, there's no need to rush". She knew he had passed away.

She loved my father like her own father and that meant a lot to me.

My father had passed away very peacefully with me there. My mother and sister come rushing in about 45 seconds later. They had seen all the nurses in the room.

My wife comes in about 3 minutes later.

My father did not deserve to go through what he went through with the disease that he had, and as much as I miss him, it was good for him that he went peacefully and did not linger on in that state for years as former President Reagan did. I know my father is in heaven looking down on me and my mother and my wife and children. I know that he's at peace, the peace that we all work for, whether we know it or not, to get to heaven. He accomplished it, through good times and bad. My father would never say anything bad about anybody, never cursed, was very humble and was a very giving person, to his children, his wife, especially my wife and children. He was a good man, a role model to many. My father never bragged, never boasted, he was very humble.

I read the readings at the funeral with my daughter and nephew standing besides me. My mother did not want me to break down reading. I thought that I would be OK and I was.

Sometimes I look up to heaven and say "I miss you dad but I'm proud of what you accomplished in life."

# Chapter Ten

We were living in our house a few months and we still couldn't find a house that my mother could buy or one that we could add on to.

She still wanted her independence, she did not want to live with us. The real estate agent who sold us our house lives next door to us and he knew my parents since he took them with us to look at houses. We told him that we were looking for a house in this neighborhood so that my mother could be closer to us. His house just happens to have an in-law house in back of his house. He told us that he might be willing to sell it if he could find another house. His wife wanted to move badly.

This sounded good to me. We went and looked at his house, my wife, my mother and my sister and me. The in-law house was small but I thought it would do. My mother said no, the whole house was too big.

There was a two story house down the block from us that was for sale. We went down and looked at it. My mother is in her early 70's and has always lived in a one story house, said that she couldn't walk up and down the stairs everyday, so that one was out.

The real estate agent, Emile Tujaque, sent out a letter to everyone on our block saying that he had a customer who was interested in buying a house on this block, is anyone interested in selling?

Now get this! The next day the people who live across the street, one house over from us said they might be interested in selling if they could find another house. They found another house and they sold their house to my mother across the street from us!

Tell me that GOD did not have anything to do with the whole situation starting with my accident!

That was omen # 11.

All things happen for a reason, whether you know the reason or not. The reason my mother did not buy his house was because it was not right for her. We had no idea she would buy the house across the street from us. The reason she did not buy the house down the block was because she wanted to live across the street from us, and that house was too big as well as being a two story house. We did not know that she would buy the house across the street, we never knew that but I was trying to force her into buying both houses. She was able to get exactly what she prayed for and that was a separate house from us and right by us.

Sometimes you do not know the reason things work out the way they do, but there is always a reason, whether you know it or not!

So my mother bought that house and unfortunately she had a lot of work to do to it. She had to buy all new appliances, re-do the kitchen, had new windows put in, she had the whole house painted, she re-did the whole house, from the inside, out.

My mother always said that our house was perfect for her but we did not want to move OR fix up another house.

Well, she fixed up her whole house with the help of my sister and if she was to sell it now she would make a nice profit. She doesn't plan on selling it but that shows you the power of prayer. She has always prayed for different things and has a close relationship with GOD. Most all of what she has prayed for has come true!

If my father was still with us, he would never have agreed to buy that house, not that I would want my father to pass away so my mother could buy that house, but it just shows you how and why things work out the way they do.

I know the power of prayers, just take my car accident and recovery for example.

About a week after my father passed away we had a hurricane come towards New Orleans and we had to evacuate. It was a strong hurricane. It took us thirteen hours to get to Texas which is the only place we could get a hotel room.

Normally, it would take us an hour to get to Baton Rouge, which is the next big city to our west; it took us FOUR hours to get their!

If my father was still with us he would have been in the nursing home; we would not have left him there, but we couldn't take him with us.

What would we have done?

So you see, whether you know the reason or not, things always work out for the better. Whether you do not even know or do not even know to know, things always work out the way they do for a reason. Whether you know or accept the reason or are not even aware of what is going on, there is a reason.

Don't fool yourself and think that things happen because you were there at the right time or you weren't there at that particular time, there is a reason why you are there or you are not there.

There is a MASTER PLAN.

Somebody knows what is going to happen to all of us every minute of every day. The plan is already set and I don't think GOD lets things happen by chance, good or bad, life is just running it's course, it's pre-planned course.

I stayed out of work for a couple of weeks to help my mother and my sister take care of business.

Getting all the paperwork changed to just my mother's name was quite an experience.

Like I said, my mother at that time had bought the house across the street from us and it needed a lot of re-modeling. The kitchen was a mess. She had all the appliances taken out and new ones installed, but not before she had a contractor come in and redo the whole house, with painting every room, putting down new carpet and wood floors and having new vanities and mirrors put in the bathrooms. She along with my sisters help, (my sister has taken interior designing courses), re-did the whole inside of the house and now it looks great.

Doing that as well as changing all the names on my parents accounts to my mother's name, was really a job, but it was something that had to be done.

My mother had to go out and buy a new dining room set, which she wanted and a file cabinet and a few other things but all in all, the house is perfect for her and I'm glad of that.

Now that my wife and I had bought another house and my mother had bought the house across the street from us, what more can you ask for.

I know that's what my father would have wanted and now, if anything happens with my mother, we are right across the street AND she gets to see her grandchildren a lot more.

So all in all, with my father leaving us, this is the best thing that could have happened for all of us.

What would make my mother really happy is if my sister and her family moved down to New Orleans from New Jersey, but we'll wait and see what happens with that one.

Once we moved in to our new house, the first person we met in the neighborhood was a man named Lee. Lee is a very nice man who my wife also gets along with (my wife has the personality that she gets along with everyone and she just drawers people towards her). Lee's wife is Barbara, and she is also very nice, and my mother gets along with both of them so it's twice as good for my mother.

In fact, when my father passed away, Lee along with his wife came to the funeral, which I thought was very nice.

We, my wife and I had just really met Lee and Barbara a few short months before (maybe two months).

Also at my fathers wake, my friend Darren Vicknair, who lives a long ways from my house and who's birthday is the same day as mine, who used to spend quite a few weekends at my house during high school, couldn't make the funeral so he told his parents and they came to the wake and funeral and that meant quite a lot to me. Along with so many friends of my parents and mine who came and sent flowers, two people from work who work inside the Post Office, came to the wake on their lunch hour to pay respect to ME, and they did not even know my father. That shows what kind of character some people have. Their names are Mary and Trudy. I was so surprised to see them that my eyes watered, and that meant a lot to me.

At the funeral, myself, my nephew, my nephew from my wife's family, my friend Louis, my brother-in-law and my son, we all carried my father's casket at church; my son is struggling to carry it (he's only eight) but he is trying and that's what counts.

I read the readings at the mass and had my nephew and my daughter came up and stand besides me to give me moral support, which I needed.

I am so proud of my daughter and son for the way they handled the whole situation with my father passing away.

It showed a whole lot of maturity and my wife and I are very proud of both of them!

Getting back to my mother's house, it fits her just fine. It has a 2 car garage and the washing machine and dryer are in the garage whereas at her last house she had to go outside to another part of the house to wash clothes. I know my father would be well pleased with the house and what my mother and sister have done to it.

My father and his sister, Bridget, my aunt, in 1991.

My mother, father, and me right before he went in a home.

My mother, father with my son and daughter.

My father giving his grandson a kiss. His grandson was one of six who carried my father's casket. It was a moving sight.

My daughter, Amber, and my grandfather.

# Chapter Eleven

As the year went along without my father, my mother is learning to do things for herself because when my father was with her, he did everything. My father was from the OLD SCHOOL, which is not bad but it was different back then. The man of the family usually did everything, now my mother had to learn everything and she is learning just fine.

She ask's me different things sometimes and I give her my opinion and let her make the decision herself. She usually makes the right decision, she is very conscience that she has to make the right decision because she will have to pay again if she makes the wrong decision. Paying again I mean if she tries to save money and do it cheap the first time, she'll have to pay to have it done right the next time.

My mother is like my wife in that she does not rush a decision, she see's what's available to her, wait's and then, and only then, she makes the decision, which is usually the right decision.

She is like my wife in that she thinks about every decision she has to make.

Another thing that I do since my father passed away is keep more in touch with my father's sister, my aunt. I know he would want this. I would call her every few weeks when my father was still here but now I try and call her at least once a week just to see how everything is going with her.

She has no family, just friends that she has spent her whole life knowing. She likes to hear from her niece and nephew (my son and daughter) and it makes me feel good to hear her voice AND I know my father would be pleased with that.

My father was very FAMILY oriented, just like my wife is. I guess that's why my father loved my wife like his own daughter, and I guess that's why my wife loved my father like her own father.

My aunt is the last of the SCANNAVINO'S, that I know to be of our family. The last time I checked there was 52 families in the United States with my last name but she is the last one that is in my family and I know that my father wants me to stay in touch with her, although I would, even if my father was still with us, and that is because my wife is so family oriented that it just rubs off on me to know my family as much as I can.

It's so hard for me to remember who is a cousin or nephew or niece with my wife's family, but I can say that I'm trying and that's good. All I know is that when I am with her family, and there's a lot of people around, I know they are all related somehow.

My aunt is so much like my wife too, in that she is so family oriented, just like my father was. She knows all about her family, who is who, what year my father went to WWII, were he went during the war, what years he was where he was, who's cousins of who, etc.. She can tell you what year something happened in the family, it's almost like she has a photogenic mind, she remember's everything about her family.

My mothers mother (my grandmother) was a tailor when she came from Italy as was my mothers grandfather and my mothers grandfather was a designer also. A tailor is someone who puts the lining in clothes, designed clothes, it was totally different from a seamstress. She was very sought after in the United States but she was busy designing clothes and raising her family that she never thought to pursue that particular trade.

Mt fathers sister was a seamstress who worked in a factory her whole life. It was so different back then. Now I don't even know if they make clothes in the United States, they all probably come from across the ocean. How the world changes.

My whole family used to drive to New York every summer and we would spend one week with my fathers family and the next week with my mothers family. I probably saw all that was important to see in New York at an early age.

One year we saw the World's Fair when it was in New York, we saw the Statue of Liberty, The Twin Towers, It is so awesome to go to the top of the Twin Towers and the Statue of Liberty and look down, the cars and people walking on the cement looked like ants, very small ants at that. We went to Coney Island, had Nathon's hot dogs, we did so much in New York. It was a very educating experience for me. I would like to take my children, I really shouldn't say children, my daughter is almost 16 and my son is almost a teenager, there more often like I did but we have to divide our vacation time between New York and New Jersey, where my sister lives with her family, and Michigan where my wife is from and something we do as a family every third year. It's different when you have a family who's parents come from two states. You have to divide the vacation time up to keep everyone happy.

We enjoy it though, rotating our vacations.

I really like investing in stocks and mutual funds so the first year my wife and I went to New York, we made it a point to go to Wall Street and see where the action is as far as making money goes. We went to a play, China Town, to see the Twin Towers and the Statue of Liberty, The Empire State Building, we even had someone take our picture of us standing on the Statue of Liberty with one of the Twin Towers behind me and the other tower behind my wife. The Twin Towers were bombed and destroyed, what a show of hatred towards our country.

That picture means a lot to me and probably to a lot of people.

I can tell my teenagers what was once the tallest towers in America and show them a picture of the Twin Towers.

So anyway, my father passed away and the next week there was a hurricane coming towards New Orleans like I said. The rest of the year did not start off on a good note, but it couldn't get any worse, we thought.

We tried to get hotel rooms anywhere but they were all booked up and the only place we could get rooms was in Houston.

We stayed on the road in bumper to bumper traffic all day. When we arrived at the hotel, they tell us that they only have one room for us!

This is after booking two rooms in advance!

The people who were ahead of us in the check-in line, changed there mind because the room smelled like smoke.

What luck, we got their room!

The hotel gave us their room.

That was omen # 12.

We get back from evacuating for the hurricane and my sister stayed with my mother for about four weeks. They were doing things to the house, getting drapes and different appliances. I'm sure it was good for my mother having her daughter there when we got back from Houston.

My sister eventually had to go since she had a family to go back to.

My mother seemed to be doing O.K., she was getting on with her life and doing quite well.

# Chapter Twelve

The next year the big one came, Hurricane Katrina and Hurricane Rita, a one, two punch.

That was history being made in America and I am sure everyone knows a little about those hurricanes.

My wife and my mother had been watching the weather station on T.V. for days, tracking the hurricanes. It was Friday night and my wife said to me," what do you want to do about the hurricane coming towards us". I said that on Saturday watch the news and whatever you and my mother decided to do, call me on my cell phone since I would be working and I will do whatever they decided.

I would be working and not be able to watch the news although the hurricane had a pretty good chance of hitting New Orleans directly.

So Saturday comes, and I am a mailman and I go out on the street at about 9:20 a.m. and my wife calls me at about 11:30. She says that she and my mother decided that we should evacuate as soon as I get home. I said that's fine, I can probably be home around 1:15.

All morning long I am hurrying on my mail route, flying from one spot to the next.

I skip my lunch and breaks and fly through my route to get home so we can leave.

I get home at 1:30 and take a shower, help finish packing the car and my wife, daughter, son and mother and the dog and cat take off to a city called Farmerville, which is about 35 miles north of Monroe which is up in the North Western part of the La. My wife's nephew, Brian Hartman lives up there and he said that we could stay with him if we wanted.

We knew we couldn't get a hotel so we took him up on his offer.

We stayed there a total of four weeks and it was so nice.

Everyone there was so nice and polite. It was like the town in the Andy Griffith show, called "Mayberry".

Everyone there just couldn't treat you well enough. The people at the bank, the people at the stores we went to, the beauticians my mother went to, the people at the Post Office, everyone was super nice AND it wasn't because we evacuated the hurricane, that's just the way they were.

There was a "recreation center" that would serve three meals a day for the evacuees. The breakfast was simple things to eat like cereal and fruit snacks but the lunch and dinner; they were four and five course meals, and they didn't just give you one serving, you could go back for more until you were full. It was really special.

They made us and all the evacuees feel like FAMILY and we appreciated that.

The first week we were there my wife inquired about enrolling our son and daughter in a school because we did not know how long we would be there.

It just so happens that the school we enrolled them in was a few blocks away from where we were staying. The school board, which we had to go to enroll our son and daughter GAVE my son uniforms to wear as well as the books he would need, and they gave him a card to get his lunch free every day; they made my son feel like he went there his whole life.

My son makes friends easy and being in a different environment really doesn't matter that much to him. He adjust's really easy and good, so that made it easier for us, his parents.

We enrolled my daughter in the same school, it was a grammar school as well as a high school.

The grammar school was a set of buildings on one side of the street and the high school was across the street.

Our daughter tends to be a little shy and the first day we dropped her off she was walking slowly inside the school. She said that when she went in, quite a few of her classmates walked up to her and hugged her and said they were glad she was there, boys and girls did that!

What a place to evacuate to!

That made the transmission to a different school a lot easier for our daughter.

One of the friends she made plays in a rock and roll band as well as a Christian band. He made a C.D. of his music and gave it to her and when we finally left to go home she was listening to it on her C.D. player in the backseat and when my wife looked back in the mirror to see her, my wife said tears where streaming down her face.

That was one of the good friends she made over there.

She made some good friends while we were there and she didn't want to leave.

She misses the friends she made up there, both boys and girls.

She still E-Mails them on the computer and talks to them on the phone; we are so proud of her and her new friends.

My mother made quite a few friends at the recreation center that we would go to. She would talk to the same ones everyday and a few had something in common in that they were religious.

At dinner time, she would always walk around talking to different people and seeing if there was anything she could do to help.

My wife was the same way, always looking to help, which was only right since these people were giving so much of their time and money to the people who evacuated.

It was so easy making friends there, so different from where we come from.

It was an honest and friendly and laidback lifestyle that we enjoyed a whole lot and will never forget it.

My wife, she makes friends wherever she goes, she just has a very nice AND honest personality. She is very sincere in everything she does, which is a rare rare today.

She drawers people towards her with her personality.

People know that when they are talking to her, what she says is how she feels. She always has something good to say or nothing to say at all.

I'm glad I was able to meet her and eventually marry her because I know I am changing for the better because of her, however slowly it is.

I always tell her my job is to make her happy and I mean that but she just thinks I'm joking.

When I met my wife she was friends with my former girlfriend, and they, along with other girls, would go out on the town sometimes, to different bars.

I had no interest in her as a girlfriend at that time, just as a friend. Eventually I broke up with my girlfriend and went out with different girls still occasionally going out with my former girlfriend, as we stayed friends, and eventually I started going out with my wife and eventually we got married.

Did you follow all of that?

It's funny the way things work out sometimes.

So we finally came back home, my wife and I, the second to last day that the parish would remain open since there was still no electricity and few places near bye were open.

They would close the parish the next day not letting any one come back in, and start to restore the power, they would start to remove the trees and debris from the street and start fixing the streets, which some were cracked and broken.

We thought that we would be able to see our house and pull up out as much of the carpet as possible and do the same thing to my mothers house.

We arrived at our house at 6:00 A.M. BUT we couldn't start pulling out carpet or emptying the refrigerator until it was light enough to see. All the electricity was out; it was like going to a ghost town, it was too dark to see. We couldn't see anything.

All the stores and gas stations were closed as well as the street lights and the store lights were not on. It was almost pitch black.

You did not see cars driving around, see people on the streets, there was no street lights, nothing! It looked like the city had been bombed and it was VACANT!

It was like a ghost town !

We had brought flashlights, knifes to cut the carpet with, we bought six gallon gasoline cans filled for my car because I did not know how much gas I had in my car and I knew the gas stations were closed; we were trying to be prepared.

We also took masks with us to wear for we assumed the smell would be terrible; no electricity for the refrigerator, which it was.

We took everything with us that we could think of that we would need.

We wound up taking carpet out of the three bedrooms and the den, then we emptied out the refrigerator.

What a smell! It literally STUNK!

Food being in there for ten days without electricity!

There was blood dripping out of the door from the meat that was in there, the eggs stunk; everything was bad, and the odor; it would just make you barf!

We had to take everything out of the refrigerator and put it in a plastic bag and tie it up. Then we left the door to the refrigerator open and put boxes of baking soda in to absorb the odor.

Wishful thinking, it did not do much for the odor.

Then we went to my mothers house and took out the two big throw mats and emptied her refrigerator.

It did not look like she got any water in her house because we did not see any mold but when we came back home for good, we saw about two inches of mold; the water had been pushed in threw the weep holes outside of the house!

What a mess emptying the refrigerators was. It was so nasty smelling that I almost had to go outside and throw up!

My wife brought her digital camera with her and between our house and my mothers house she took about two hundred pictures for our insurance company.

We did what we could in the amount of time that we had, but under the circumstances, we still had to drive around seven hours and stop to get something to eat!

We probably left around 3:00 that afternoon and headed back to our nephews house.

We drove on the highway for about ten miles expecting to get back on the interstate once we passed a big portion of the damage that the hurricane had done and all the traffic that we thought would be there.

Guess again!

It must have taken us around three hours to go ten miles on the highway!

We finally got back on the interstate and stopped somewhere along the way to get something to eat.

We stopped at a "Shony's" to get something to eat and all they had was the salad bar. Not bad considering the circumstances.

We did not get back to my nephew's house until around ten thirty at night.

What a day that was!

Even after taking a shower, we still smelled like the food in the refrigerator. It took days to get rid of that smell on us!

# Chapter Thirteen

The whole time we were up there in Farmerville, the recreation center took great care of all the evacuees.

They told us how to get Red Cross benefits, even took us to the place where the Red Cross was set up to get the benefits.

They told us how to apply for F.E.M.A. benefits and took us to apply for the benefits.

They told anyone who would be eligible for unemployment where to go to apply for benefits.

They were happy to do all this, in addition to feeding us.

There was probably 200 evacuees there and they made enough food for everyone.

When we went to mass on Sunday, the only Catholic church just happened to be a few miles away!; after mass they had a BIG meal for all the evacuees. Every where we went, there was food for you to eat. The people expected you to eat or they would feel bad.

I don't mean just sandwiches, I mean cooked meals to eat with dessert.

Everybody was so nice and polite.

It almost made you feel like you weren't good enough to be fed by the people there because they were so nice and you felt that you weren't good enough to be treated with such respect.

My wife did not want to go to the recreation center at first, she thought it was for people less fortunate than we were. One day I was talking to this man who happened to work at the recreation center and he insisted that we should go, that all they were doing was for all the evacuees, rich and poor.

That made my wife feel better and I know she is glad that we did go there because we made some really good and special friends.

GOD does work in mysterious ways

You just never know what HE has in store for you.

When we went there, at first we felt kind of like we were hypocrites. We were not poor and weren't in need and we felt that they were doing this for the less fortunate ones but after a couple of days we felt like we belonged there. We started to make friends especially my wife and mother. All of us, my children included, were on first name basis with almost everyone there. My mother became friends with a lady who worked at the recreation center, and this lady had to go to the hospital and my mother was worried about her. She asked her if it would be alright if she prayed for her and the lady said yes.

When that lady was in the hospital, my mother asked another lady how the lady in the hospital was doing every day. They became friends and both of them believed in GOD and what HE can do for you.

Her name was Sue and she was very nice.

My mother also made friends with the librarian at the school were my children went and they remained friends.

Another lady who was also nice, (all of the people there were nice but these I remember the most), Bettye, always asked me when my family and I were moving up there. It was a joke.

I don't think a day went by when she didn't ask me that question. She even said she new someone who would help me find a house.

She was another one who was very nice, everyone there, not only at the recreation center, but everywhere, was so nice.

The thing was, they weren't just doing this to impress us, but everyone was nice and polite, the kids, people who worked at the stores, beauticians, people who worked at the Post Office, banks, restaurants, everyone was nice and polite!

I don't mean to leave anyone out but there is just too many people to mention.

Everyone was so nice it's just too hard to name everyone without forgetting someone.

I know I'm repeating myself but the way people treated my family and me was something we will never forget!

The whole city from the people who worked at the bank, the store, the pizza shop, the car dealership (which I went to more than once because of car trouble and never paid a penny to have it fixed), the Barber shop, even strangers on the street; they were just so nice, it was like nothing I or my family or mother had never seen.

My wife had seen it at home in Michigan in the city she lived in because everyone was just as nice.

I just can't say enough nice things about the city!

It was just a very nice, extremely polite city and one we will never forget.

THANK-YOU Farmerville for all you did for us. We will never forget you and you will always be in our prayers.

One of the friends my daughter made there, the one who played guitar in a band, is coming to our city this summer and they already made plans for him to come by our house.

He'll be staying with family not too far from our house and they already made plans on seeing each other a lot.

My daughter made some really good friends there and I hope they are life long friends because it was a good experience for her.

It just shows you that there are different people everywhere, people who really care about you and how you are doing.

I think one of the reasons we wound up in Farmerville was because GOD wanted us to go there, because of my wife's nephew, to see first hand the way people can and should act and treat each other. To really take an interest in how other people are doing and to help other people, especially strangers, to treat people you don't know the way you would want to be treated by different people.

It is like one of the TEN COMMANDMENTS, treat others like you would like to be treated.

I truly believe that the way the people acted in Farmerville was sincere, that the way they acted was genuine, true. They act that way every day and I miss that, I miss the way people treat other people for our children's sake and my sake.

It was truly a good experience for all of us.

Going to Farmerville was omen # 13.

# Chapter Fourteen

We were up in Farmerville when the hurricane hit New Orleans and just watching the damage and destruction that was thrown upon New Orleans on T.V.; we couldn't believe it. There were people stranded in New Orleans with no way out. These were mostly poor, older people with some white and Latino and black people with no way to evacuate, they were stranded there with no way out.

The day after the hurricane hit we saw people stranded in the Supedome and the Convention Center with nothing to eat or drink. People were starting to walk along the interstate trying to get out, but to where were they to go? The people had nothing to eat or drink, no shelter from the weather, thank GOD it was not cold or worse, raining, no place to go to the bathroom, it was mass CHAOS!

The people were looking for help but none was in site.

The Governor and the Mayor had no communication between them, it was a lack of total communication between the local and federal government.

I don't know if communication would have done any good, because it seemed like they could not handle the situation that was thrown at them.

I don't know if anyone could have handled it any better, but I think that an evacuation should have been ordered well in advance of the hurricane and that food and water should have been brought in by helicopter the next day for the stranded people.

Nobody should have to go through that kind of humiliation.

After a few days the President stepped up to the plate and called for F.E.M.A to come in and help. Also the National Guard came to help, which was desperately needed. Finally they started bringing food for the people to eat and water to drink and busses came to bring the people out of town, mostly to the state of Texas, our next door neighbor, and what a wonderful job they did for New Orleans!

Texas along with numerous other states took in thousands of people who left New Orleans and what a terrific job they did for New Orleans!

They will never be forgotten for what they did for the people of New Orleans.

They opened their arms and gave the evacuees housing and food and clothes, even toys for the children. It brings a tear to my eye as well as many other citizens of the state of Louisiana as well as the United States to see so many people opening up their hands and WALLETS to help when some kind of disaster strikes.

It was kind of like the support the country gave New York when 9/11 occurred.

It was that kind of charity from everyone that helped New Orleans dig its way out of the disaster.

# Chapter Fifteen

The next day we still had our work cut out for us. We had to find a company who would remove the mold and get the smelly water out and remedy the situation. We didn't know where to start looking for mold remediation companies.

We got on the computer and looked for mold remediation.

We found a few companies and we called them all only to find that we were put on a waiting list for all except one. We were able to talk to one company and another company called us back. We were told to look at this one companies web page and to read it, it explained all you needed to know about the company and what they did.

We read that page and it sounded good to us. It said what the company did to remove the mold and how they treated the house, the only problem was they already had a waiting list of eight weeks to see your house. We couldn't wait that long. The mold would be up to the ceiling by then.

The other company called us back and they seemed to know what to do and how to do it so we made an appointment for them to come out to our house and look at our problem, which wasn't unique, since almost everyone had water which in turn produced the mildew.

We told them that we were still evacuated and they said they would be in our neighborhood on a certain date and we said that we would be there to meet them.

We were still in Farmerville deciding when to leave, but there was just one problem, another hurricane was coming towards Louisiana. They still did not know where it was going to hit but it did not look good for New Orleans.

My wife, the one who ALWAYS thinks ahead, said why don't we wait until after the hurricane hits, wherever it hits, so we don't have to drive back only to have to evacuate again.

So we waited until the hurricane hit and then drove back.

The hurricane, this one named "Rita" hit the lower south west corner of the state where Louisiana meets up with Texas.

We were sparred this time, thank goodness. We did not need to get another drenching and wind damage, although some people said that we had already suffered from one, another one wouldn't do that much damage. I guess it is just the way look at things.

So, we were sparred from this one and what a relief that was.

We left the next day in our two cars on the long trip home.

We drove back and had to stop to pick up my wife's sister's mother-in-law who had evacuated also and was staying with some of her relatives not to far from Farmerville

She was in a city not to far from us and we met her at a doughnut shop to bring her back with us. She had gotten a ride there with her grandson who had since left and we had to drop her off at my sister-in-law's house.

My wife's sister had been looking at our house and relaying the message to us in Farmerville as well as a neighbor who lives down the street from us. We were getting information from two different people, which was good.

We left my sister-in-laws house and went to our house; there wasn't anything we could do except look at it, we couldn't sleep in it, there was no electricity; we went back to my sister-in- laws house with my mother and settled down for a rather extended stay there.

They have a big three story house and they put up my family as well as my mother, my sister-in-laws sister-in-law(do you understand that one!), my sister-in-laws mother-in-law; at one time we had 12 people in this one house. The thing was, nobody knew how long they would be there!

My sister in law did not care.

My sister-in-law's sister-in-law's house was in a city called Lakeview and a lot of the houses there got from three feet of water to being covered with water. They did not know when they would be leaving.

My sister-in-laws mother-in-laws house was in New Orleans; she didn't suffer hardly any water damage because her house is a raised enough to park a car under the house but she did suffer some wind damage, she had no electricity or gas, she did not know when she would be allowed to return home.

Our house was simply unlivable and we did not know when we would be able to return.

Then in two days, we met the mold re-mediation company and we walked through our house with them.

They told us what they would do and explained to us how long it would take to do the whole process.

We decided to hire them and they came back with the papers for us to sign. My mother decided to sign the papers to do her house also since she too had a few inches of mold growing up her walls by this time. So my mother signed on the dotted line for them to remove her mold and we also signed on the dotted line for them to do our house.

The good thing was, the company said they would take our deposit and that they then would take whatever our insurance company payed them, they would handle all the paper work. Sounded good to me and my wife as well as my mother.

All three of us read the papers, signed them then wrote a check for our deductible amount and that was that. We were set.

They decided to do our house first since we had more water which resulted in more mold. They first took out the rest of the carpet that was left in the house along with the carpet pads. Next came pulling out all of the kitchen appliances, cabinets and counter tops, then they moved to the bathrooms, again they had to take everything out except the bathtub and the only reason that stayed was because they were one piece tubs and showers and no mold could grow on the shower. Next they took out four feet of Sheetrock out throughout the house since we had mold that was 18-20 inches high.

After they finished taking everything out, they sprayed a formula on the walls to kill the mold and mopped the entire floor with a mold killer formula. Then they dehumidified the whole house with de-humidifier machines in every room as well as fans in every room. The whole process took seven days and we were satisfied with the whole process, we thought, until the insurance adjuster came to our house which wasn't for a few weeks.

They were finished with the whole house, except there were no wallsfrom four feet down in the house, you could see throughout the entire house.

So now we had to wait for the insurance adjuster to come out to our house to see the damage.

The first adjuster to come to our house was the homeowners adjuster. The homeowners insurance covers whatever wind damage you have, which was a lot for us. We had about a third of the roof shingles blown off the roof, and we were on the list to get a "blue roof" from F.E.MA., then a part of our wooden fence was blown down, then the mailbox, which is by the street was blown down breaking the concrete that held it in the ground. Next there was part of the fascia that was blown off, and last but not least, we had two trees in front of our house that both were blown down leaning against our house, and roof.

Our house was pretty well damaged from the wind, but just wait until the flood adjuster comes to our house because flood insurance covers ALL water damage to your property, inside and outside.

That homeowners adjuster was from Texas and I guess he stayed about 30 minutes, it really did not take him long to access the damage.

So know there was nothing we could really do except wait for the next adjuster to come to our house, (the flood adjuster).

While we were waiting for the flood adjuster to come, we started looking for a contractor to rebuild our house but trying to find one was a job in itself. A neighbor of ours who owns a T.C.B.Y. recommended one that she used in her shop whenever she needed something done.

My wife was home because her job as a nursery school teacher was no more because of the flood; she would eventually go back with a promotion when they fixed the school from all the water damage it suffered but for now she was home and could take care of all the jobs related to rebuilding our house. She called the contractor our neighbor recommended and had him come over and look at our house, which was good because I had went back to work after four weeks, and we still had some mail carriers out because of the hurricane, and I would not be able to do all the work as far as finding a contractor, telling them what we wanted done and so on.

He went home that night and wrote up a proposal stating what was going to be done and in what stages it would be done in.

We both looked at his proposal and agreed on it; he knew that it would be a while before we received the insurance money and he knew that before he started, which was good for us.

I'll jump forward two weeks. The flood adjuster came to our house at a scheduled time of 2:00; he did not leave until 6:30, 4 1/2 hours later!

He went in every room first and measured it. We told him what was in every room and even gave him a D.V.D. with all the pictures that my wife had taken when we came in to pull the carpet up. He told us what the mold re-mediation company had NOT done when taking out the Sheetrock. My wife had a big mirror on back of the bathroom closet door, they threw it away with the door. The mirror was not damaged by mold so why through it away? They should have taken the mirror of the door before throwing the door away! The doors, each one in the house needed to be thrown away but the doorknobs were still good, why did they throw them away with the doorknobs still on them, why not take the door knobs off?

There were things that we did not know about but this was the first case of mold that we had to deal with, so we were naive about it.

We had made two piles of the contents from the house that we divided in back of our house. We showed him the two piles, one that we were going to keep and one that we were going to throw away.

He looked at the A.C. in the backyard and it was sitting in water and he gave us credit for that, our shed in the backyard was under water and so was our lawnmower, he gave us credit for the lawnmower and shed.

He seemed to be very fair but we will tell when we get the settlement, which we haven't as of the writing of this book.

We were told by our insurance company to keep a part of the carpet to show the adjuster and we did that as well as keep a portion of the wood from the wood floor as well.

When this adjuster came out to the house, it was already being put back in order, although it would be some time before it was ready to move back to.

So, anyway, back to the house.

We had all the Sheetrock and insulation put back in, we had some walls moved; we painted all the walls and all the ceilings, the house was SLOWLY taken shape, but it will be a long time before we can move back in.

We went to a bathroom store were they surround your bathtub with marble. It was a nice store, nice fixtures to look at and get ideas, and we picked out a new bathtub since ours was a one piece tub-shower and it was an ugly yellow and my wife said that we should re-do the bathroom now since everything was taken out and nothing that we were adding to it would match yellow, but when we went to the sales lady, she said that they could put our name on their list but it would be four months before someone could call us to come out to our house and measure for the marble. That's how busy these places were since the hurricane hit us.

We put our name on the list and probably will wait unless we find a different place that can do it sooner.

They put the ceramic floor in our house; in the kitchen, breakfast area and the garage, they came and put the wood down in our foyer and living room and hallway, they will be putting the carpet in the bedrooms in about a week. The only thing left is the kitchen with its appliances, cabinets and counter tops and the bathrooms. Your guess is as good as mine when that will get done.

In addition to that, whenever we do get the full settlement from the insurance company, the insurance company puts the name of our mortgage company and our name on the check so we have to sign the check then send it to the mortgage company to sign it then they send it back to us.

Where we live we get our mail from the main Post Office which is in New Orleans and that Post Office was flooded from the hurricane!

So let me explain. If a company sends me a piece of mail from anywhere in the United States, it doesn't get here in two or three days like it used to take. Now the letter that used to go to New Orleans now goes to a different city, that city has it's own mail to sort out and can't do our mail so they send the mail to a different city and that city sends it to a different city which sorts the mail out for us, that city, after it is finished sorting the mail sends it back to the city that the mail went to before going there then that city sends it to the city it went to before it went there and from there it is finally driven to our Post Office. All this takes about two or more weeks.

I hope you followed that because it's hard to understand. That is how us and our neighboring city's who received their mail from New Orleans gets their mail. It is not hard to understand if you know that we received our mail from New Orleans and that Post Office is no longer there as of the writing of this book. It will be rebuilt, like the rest of the city but that takes time and nobody has time. I can say this, the Post Office is doing all it can to take care of people's mail and get it to them as fast as we can.

Also, when the insurance company sends you the check and you have to send it to the mortgage company to sign, they in turn send you a portion of the check to fix your house and they will send you some more money as the work get's done to your house!

So you can see how long this process is, it can literally take four or five months or longer to get your house fixed up!

So the purpose of me telling you that is TIME, it takes time to get your check from the insurance company then send it to your mortgage company and then have them endorse it and send it back to you, it's a slow process.

In addition to waiting for the check from the mortgage company, they do not simply sign it and send it back to you, that would be too easy. They send an inspector to your house to see how much improvement you have done to your house and then they write you a check ONLY for a percentage of the improvements you have done!

So you have to keep receiving a check, signing it and sending it to your mortgage company only to have them send an inspector to your house to see how much work has been done.

It is a very time consuming process.

So anyway, we are still staying with my sister-in-law and her husband and we couldn't ask for anyone better to stay with (except Farmerville). They have been spectacular. My sister-in-law always cooks dinner, we have our own bedroom and our children have there own bedroom, we brought our computer over there so this is where I am writing part of this book, we brought our treadmill over here and my daughter uses it, they have a poolroom where my son likes to play pool. Our children have a T.V. up in their room so they can watch T.V. whenever they want, it just couldn't have worked out any better. My wife gets to spend time with her sister and brother-in-law, she is so family oriented that it worked out good for her. Everything worked out the way it was planned out by our CREATOR.

A few years ago, Tom and Jeannie, my wife's brother-in-law and sister, used to live in another state; if they still lived there we would not be able to stay with them.

I believe this is how GOD wanted it, for us to get to know Jeannie and Tom a little better (although we both knew them but not on a day to day basis) and see how they live, HE wanted us to see that and how good it is and give my wife some time with her sister.

So we've been staying there for two months as of the writing of this book, and the book is still not done.

It's a slow process and there is nothing you can do to speed it up.

It is a slow process for everyone involved. We have someone to stay with and sleep and they are in no rush to see us go but what about the people who don't have family to stay with? I work with some people who lost everything, the whole house, their car, all family belongings, everything, AND they still have a house payment to make! What do they do?

We don't have it as bad as it could be, as you can see, but it still bad for us.

Our mortgage company suspended our payments until we move back and get back on our feet.

It's all working out good for us.

We and the people who live here will rebuild, it may take some time, but we will rebuild.

GOD doesn't give you anything you can't handle although at the time you may think you can't handle it, sometimes you need a little help from your CREATOR.

# Chapter Sixteen

My wife has done as good a job as anyone could do under these circumstances.

She is slowly getting our house built back; we both have input as to what we want, we are both doing what we can to speed up the process and helping do what we can, and most of all, she is keeping our family together.

Our children come first, but they have to understand what is going on, and I think they do. They are being patient and understanding.

She took care of all the school situation's for them, getting them enrolled in their respective school's, keeping them entertained as much as she could.

She finally went back to work with a promotion and she loves her job. My wife was made to be with children and she is a nursery school instructor. As such, she is responsible for the schedule of the children's day and she is responsible for any feedback from the parents.

She is the main teacher and get this, she teaches little two year old students computer.

It's a kid friendly class but they are using computers!

She is just plain good.

I am lucky to have someone with a personality like that.

So our house is finally looking like a house again.

We had the workers come and put the ceramic down, they came and put the wood floor down and now we are waiting for them to put the carpet in. After that we have to wait for the people to come out for the kitchen cabinets and the counter tops, we still have to get a new roof, and last but not least, the bathrooms need to be re-done.

So our house is slowly taking shape. As of the writing of this book, it has been FIVE months.

FIVE MONTHS!

I thought by now we would have been in our house and back to life as normal.

The city would be back to normal, the schools would be back to normal, everything back to normal!

It's not and it will probably not be a long time.

I truly believe the city of New Orleans will be re-built better than before. I think that this city has to much history and cultural diversity to be anything but re-built better than before.

Remember what I said before. There is a reason that things happen, whether you know the reason or not, there is a reason.

There was a reason I had to have my accident.

Did I say HAD? Yes. There was a reason I had to have my accident and I can tell you it was a good reason. How can being in a coma for twelve days be good? Who knew I would rehabilitate as well as I did. It wasn't for the money I would get from my settlement. It wasn't that much.

How could putting your parents through such uncertainty be good?

It was, although I would never put my parents through that again, and now I know what I can do to avoid being put in that situation again!

There was a reason I had to have my accident. It was to make me a better person, take life more seriously and not be so "happy go lucky".

I'm not a great person, but my accident did make me a better person.

There was a reason why I asked that girl at the bank to call me and finally marry me AND there was a reason why she said yes.

I can honestly say that my wife has worn off on me. She is nice to everybody, she doesn't change her personality from one minute to the next. I truly believe that I married my wife to be a more responsible person, (I know my daughter would ask me to show her how I'm more responsible).

She, my wife, is happy with what has been bestowed on us and doesn't want anymore.

She is truly a great person and I'm happy she is part of my life.

There was a reason why I had to get fired from the job I loved.

The reason was that if I didn't get fired, the Post Office would have eventually called like they did, and I would have turned them down, I know I would have; I loved my job at the convenience store.

That's kind of interesting.

There is a reason why I job hoped before finally getting hired at the Post Office.

The reason was to show me that you have to work hard for what you want in life, nothing is given to you. These are my thoughts.

There is a reason why my wife and I have bought three house.

The reasons are we started a home based business and needed a bigger house. The reason we sold our second house was because we had a crazy family living next to us that made our life unlivable and second was because we were looking for a house that my parents could share with us, a house with an apartment or in-law house attached to it or one that we could add an in-law house onto it.

Although living next to that man-boy pushed our idea fast-forwarded.

There is a reason why I had that run-in with the man-boy at our second house, which I did not tell you about simply because it makes my wife throw-up whenever she hears his name mentioned.

The reason was to move sooner than expected, but it worked out good for my family that way.

There is a reason why I was able to be in the room with my father when he passed away.

I don't know the reason for that one only to say that I loved him and that I appreciated all that he and my mother have done for me through the years.

There is a reason why these things and many more things have happened.

I think I know the reason some of these things happened.

I THINK because I am not sure. I can only make an educated guess and I think I am right about this.

Yes, my accident worked out for the best for me.

How can I say that, knowing that I was in a coma for twelve days, not knowing if I would come out of it, not knowing how much I would rehabilitate, not knowing how my memory would be, not knowing how my personality would turn out?

I'm sure my wife wishes I could have turned out a little better, but all in all, I'm a descent person.

My accident turned out good for me.

How can I say that?

Well, look at the whole picture.

I'm still who I was. I really didn't change that much, I just grew older, with a little help from GOD.

Some people say that's too bad because I need to change, other people say that's good because I am a good person the way I am.

If you know me, that's a choice you will have to make.

It wasn't for the money, I still have to work and help raise a family.

The money wasn't nearly enough, it's a good thing I had insurance or it would have really put a big strain on my family.

It's for all the benefits I have from a terrible tragedy, mostly the benefits I have received from my wife, which was not my wife at the time of my accident, and both of my parents, my sister Pru and her husband Michael, and my aunt Bridget. It's what I learn from my children, my daughter and son.

I learn a lot from my daughter especially and I learn from my son, but mostly I learn from my wife all the important things, like not to be jealous or envious of people and to be happy with what we have, and mostly, I learn how to talk NICE to people. I still say what I feel, but I try to talk politely all the time (I still at that one).

It's all the good that has come out of November 19, 1983, at around 2:35 a.m..

It's a day that I will never forget and I know my mother and father will never forget.

Remember, you can't keep a good man down!

# Chapter Seventeen

My daughter is now 33 and she has gone from high school to college. Her name is Amber.

She first went to LSU then went to OUR LADY OF THE LAKE and finally finished at NORTHWESTERN to become a registered nurse.

At her graduation they has a slide show that showed a student kneeling down next to a stack of nursing books.

They were four feet high!

Thick books with no pictures.

My son in law bought her a GMC Acadia. His name is Chase and he is a well educated man who does all kinds of work.

She is married now and has three children Sophia, Cohen and Jake.

My son is Christopher.

He graduated from high school and worked with my son in law doing surveying.

He did that for a year and decided to go to college. He went to a Junior College called Delgado and finished welding. Then he went to the UNIVERSITY OF New Orleans and graduated with a degree in finance and economics. He was doing fine working for a financial planner and then went to a C.P.A. firm that does business tax returns.

He is married to Patricia who has a degree in Clinical Mental Health Counseling and my son and Patricia ave two children named Christopher and Dominic.

My wife is named Sandy the handy man! Just joking its Sandy. She does so much repair work ay home for us that I call her Sandy the repair man.

# Conclusion

> I write poetry and that two of the poems
> I wrote are about my children

I would like to tell you that I really enjoyed writing this book. This is one of those things that I think I recovered from my accident so well; I think I should do my part, and that is to try and help as many people who have some kind of setback in life, be it a car accident, a disability or they are just having trouble getting in the right lane in life.

I've read many books since my accident that helps you get a better perspective on life and why some things happen.

This book was not written to be a best seller but simply to help a certain type of people.

I hope that if you do read this book that it helps you out at least a little.

I think that is one of the reasons I had my wreck and recovered the way I did, to do my part in helping people out.

If you did suffer some kind of setback, I wish you luck in coming back, and remember, it doesn't matter what you look like or how you walk, it doesn't matter if people can see that you are different or did not recover all the way to the pre-??? way you were.

It does not matter how you talk.

IT DOES NOT MATTER.

I know how it feels and it took me a LONG time to get over it.

I was extremely self conscience about the way I walked, the way I talked and my lack of normal hearing. None of these things were a natural occurrence, it was the result of my accident.

I did not ask to have my accident; if I was asked I would have asked you if you were crazy.

It did turn out to be O.K., though, I found out who my true friends were, I found out who was a fake person (the manager at the store who eventually was able to get me out of her ambitious way's (but now she doesn't have a job because the company that we both worked for was bought out and then eventually went bankrupt), I found out that sometimes you have to work for something and for me it was getting back to normal and getting a job.

I also found out that there is a superior being, GOD who watches over all of us (I knew this already). I knew there was a GOD, I believed in GOD and all that HIS son has done and I basically was a good person BUT that was as far as it went. GOD took a far back seat in my life, now I am more aware of GOD in my life.

I pray every day, I talk to GOD every day, thanking HIM for all good that happens to me, and there is a lot of good that happens to me, starting with my parents, they are the best. My whole family, my aunts and uncles and my wife, which is probably the best thing that has EVER happened to me.

I am a better person because of my accident and that's why I'm glad THAT at that time in my life, I had my accident.

I had everything going for me; my family, my youth, my friends, my doctors, everything.

It could have turned out much different.

Thank-you GOD!

Well, anyway, here's some of the poetry I have written since my high school years. As you can see, I write poems mostly about things that are personal to me, although I do write poems about anything, spur of the moment.

Here's my poems.
I hope you like them...

Russ Scannavino

You're our daughter, Amber Rose,
We love the way you smile and stand up on your toes.

We love to watch you grin and laugh at everything,
You make us so happy, we just want to sing.

We want you to know, that while you're still at home,
We'll help you to grow, and not let you roam.

You're growing up so fast, it's hard to believe,
Soon you'll be old enough, and you'll want to leave.

We want you to know, if there's anything you need,
We'll do everything that we can, to plant the seed.

And when that day comes, and you decide to leave home,
You'll still be in our hearts, and never alone.

We hope you grow up, are happy and proud,
To think of your thoughts and ideas out loud.

One day you'll have a husband, we can see that,
To love and care for, and sometimes just chit-chat.

Don't run from your troubles, go cry and pout,
Talk to each other, and it will work itself out.

We want you to know, that we care and love you so.
We want you to be happy, prosper and grow.

Good luck with your family, friends and foes,
You'll still be are daughter, Amber Rose.

A Second Chance

*October 13, 1990*

This poem is about my son.

Christopher, Christopher, you're over a year now,
You're starting to walk, get around and sometimes we say,
"Christopher, how...

Christopher, Christopher, when you don't get your way,
You rant and rave, a bad part of your day.

We know it's just a matter of time for you to grow up,
So slow down, have patience, and let opportunities show up.

You're so much different than your sister was at that age,
She was so calm and peaceful, and sometimes you're full of rage.

You're a boy, she's a girl, we knew that from the start,
The way you play, the things you do, it's easy to tell you apart.

But while you're growing up, you're mother and I can see,
That you'll be mischievous, happy, and sometimes just full of glee.

When you start to go to school, we want you to know,
That we'll be there to help, and make sure you go slow.

Christopher, Christopher, don't let life pass you by,
You're young yet and playful, it's not worth it to cry.

So grow up now, be happy and do your thing,
You'll be a success, a real winner, and full of zing.

When you get married, have kids, pets and then,
Have patience, treat them right, but most of all,
Be proud of them.

Russ Scannavino

*March 29, 1995*

This is a poem I wrote for my parents back in 1992

Dear Mom and Dad,

I have so much to be thankful for,
The way you raised me and opened up the second door.

Don't think I don't appreciate all that you've done,
I'm grateful for it all, so watch me run.

You put me in the right schools and watched me achieve,
You always sat by me, let me listen, ask questions and believe.

I was a playboy of sorts,
Not a worry in the world, or so I thought.

I'd work, get paid, go out till all hours of the night,
I'd go to work, do my job, and do it right.

I'm married now and have a beautiful wife and child,
To teach and learn from and sometimes be wild.

Sometimes it seems, by the way that I speak,
That I don't care for or love you, and that's oh, so bleak.

It's easy to feel that I'm mad and don't love you so,
but read between the lines to see
That you're everything in the world to me.

I hope I'm always there for you, just like you've always been for me,
To love and care for, and sometimes just let you be.

Your son,
Rosario

A Second Chance

*June 21, 1992*

I wrote this poem for Fr. Greg Aymond who later became a Bishop. He has always been a friend of my parents and I went to the high school where he was teaching at and I think a lot of him.

Fr. Greg, a true friend

I met you in high school,
when you were starting out
as a deacon.

You taught me, tried to get me to think.

You were a light, a cornerstone, a bright deacon.

One night the student council, you and I went out
To get some pizza, I think.
We were driving back to school
I stopped, backed into your car
You were agitated I know, but it didn't show,
Because it didn't even make you blink.

I was class president one year, then the next
the treasurer of the student council.

All the while I grew into a leader, more outgoing,
and became more docile.

After high school, I went to Saint Bens,
to settle down and grow.

But after a semester there,
left, I felt I still had
some seeds to hoe.

I then went to work, was a success
in my own eyes.

I had a girlfriend, a good job
but I wasn't a where of all the lies.

When I had my near fatal accident,
you let me know
that I wasn't alone.
My car was gone,
two years of rehab.,

But I knew GOD'S work
had yet to be shown.

You married Sandy and I,
what a blessing to be,

baptized our daughter Amber
GOD'S work we could surely see.

Then you were named MSGR.
A title only for you.

You continued to do GOD'S work, were affectionate
and still "True Blue".

Next you were named Bishop
which came as no surprise.

My family and parents got to see it,
bringing tears of happiness
to our eyes.

A SECOND CHANCE

Then when you became Bishop
you were assigned to a different state,

it was time for you to leave
GOD'S work, still had to be done,
by you
I truly believe.

Russ Scannavino

Russ Scannavino

*September 28, 2000*

And now, I'd like to thank all the people who helped me and gave me support and insight into what I was writing, AND to the people who I work with who doubted me when I said that I was writing a book about my accident.

In no particular order.

To Kevin Erickson and his wife Holly. We had fun seeing each other, with our girlfriends, at the restaurant we used to go to. Thanks for being a friend Kevin.

To Al Philips. We became better friends because of my accident. Thanks Al.

To Louis Colmenares, the artist. You will always be my friend.

To David Eguidan. My assistant mgr. at work. I always admired you David and wish we could be closer.

To Darren Vicknair. You are truly a friend. Let me know if you need anything.

To Fr. Ray Hebert, Bishop Greg Aymond and Archbishop Robert Muench. I think the world of all of you. Good luck to all.

To my mother and father. I would not be here to write this book if it wasn't for you. I love you.

To my sister Prudence. Thanks for the books you gave me to read. I love you.

To Robert McGarry. Thanks for the advice you gave me when I was writing this book.

To my aunt Bridget. Thanks for the support you gave me. You and my father are so much alike.

Last but not least, my wife Sandy. You continue to give me support and encouragement. Thanks for everything you have done and will continue to do. I learn a lot from you.

And to all those I didn't mention by name who came to see me in the hospital and gave me support, I say thank's and I love all of you.

This book was written for one reason and one reason only. To give everyone who has suffered some kind of injury, be it a head injury, which I am of that class, or some kind of different injury, or just some kind of set back in life. There is always hope.

I will not say that everyone will recover like I did, which is not to say that I recovered completely, although physically I am complete, but mentally I might not be all the way there, I do not know. I do know that you do have to have hope spiritually because GOD did make you and I don't think GOD wants anything BAD to happen to anybody.

Things happen, like my car accident. I do not think GOD made my accident happen. It was just a way of life here on earth whereas people do make mistakes like driving drunk and stealing. It is just a way of life, period.

It is how you recover and how you apply your faith. I was lucky in that my mother is very religious and I know that played a very important part in the way I recovered. It was like my mother knew exactly what to do in that particular situation and I think she did everything just the way it was supposed to be done.

My father played a very important part also. Remember he was working at the time. EVERYDAY when he got off of work he would come to the hospital and see me and my mother and all of the friends that were there. Then when I was transferred to the hospital across the river, every night when he got off of work, he and my mother came twenty miles to see me. On Sunday my mother and father would drive over the river, pick me up and bring me home, then three hours later they would drive me back to the hospital to drop me off and drive back home.

My father gave me all the mental support I needed.

Both of my parents were put to the test and I think they passed with flying colors.

Fr. Ray Hebert was concerned with how I was, and this was five years after I graduated from high school, maybe seeing him once in those five years, that he came to the hospital to see me, that meant a lot.

Bishop Greg Aymond came to the hospital to see me and give me communion. That's what I call a true friend and that will never be forgotten.

All the friends who came to see me during this time, especially the ones I mentioned like David, Kevin, Al, Louis and Darren, Richie and everybody else I say thanks again, I will never forget any of you.

Like I said there was a reason why I HAD to have my accident and I can honestly say that I am happy with the results of it, the way it worked out.

If my accident did not happen I would not be able to write this book. I would not be married to my wife, I can guarantee you that and I would not have my two great children that my wife and I have, I would not be working for the Post Office; a lot of things would be different.

So yes I am glad that I had my accident (did I just say that!) not almost getting killed but with the happy results of it.

Remember there is always a reason why everything happens, whether you know the reason or not, there is a reason.


Remember, YOU CAN'T KEEP A GOOD MAN DOWN
I AM PROOF OF THAT.

# About the Author

This is the first book Russ has written but I believe he has tried to put his experience into this for the purpose of uplifting other people who have suffered the same or possibly some other kind of setback. I believe his motive is to share my recovery so that others can see that there is always HOPE

After his discharge from two hospitals, I wasn't satisfied to just sit at home doing nothing. I spent hours reading out loud to himself to improve his speech. I worked at different jobs trying to improve my interaction with others.

If anyone wants to get in touch with me contact the publisher.

www.ingramcontent.com/pod-product-compliance
Lightning Source LLC
LaVergne TN
LVHW091534070526
838199LV00001B/64